When to Advertise

When to Advertise

Simon Broadbent

Admap Publications
in association with
Incorporated Society of British Advertisers
Institute of Practitioners in Advertising

First published 1999

Admap Publications
Farm Road
Henley-on-Thames
Oxfordshire RG9 1EJ
United Kingdom
Telephone: +44 (0) 1491 411000
Facsimile: +44 (0) 1491 571188
E-mail: admap@ntc.co.uk

A CIP catalogue record for this book is available from
the British Library

ISBN 1-84116-048-2

Typeset in 11/12.7 pt Times by Admap
Printed and bound in Great Britain by
Biddles Ltd, Guildford and King's Lynn

Contents

Acknowledgements

I have worked for Leo Burnett for nearly 40 years, as a media researcher, as Media Director and as a consultant – in London, Chicago and other cities.

I have been helped by many people both in Leo Burnett and in Starcom Media Services, in discussions and with material. My thanks are due particularly to Jayne Spittler and Kate Lynch, and to Kelly Andrews, Karen Fraser, Denise Gardiner, Kathrin Haarstick, Elizabeth Hyde, Boaz Rosenberg, Regina Urbanowicz, Alice Sylvester, Megan Tarpy and Mary Ellen Vincent.

Valuable material has been contributed by Alan Smith and Dick Dodson and by Paul Dyson and Nigel Hollis of Millward Brown.

I am particularly grateful to those who played major parts in the story I tell in Part 2. They have shared their comments and insights – some of them, their biographies: Steve Coffey, Erwin Ephron, John Philip Jones, Colin McDonald, Mike Naples, Walter Reichel, Andrew Roberts and Leslie Wood. I interviewed Timothy Joyce a month before his death and Helen Joyce has read the important material he provided.

Too many media people treat – often in cavalier fashion – learning which has been hard-won by individual effort. The book is a small tribute to the insight and liberality of pioneers.

Many of these contributors have also generously helped me with suggestions and revisions. There is agreement in the industry that the subject is important and that the story should be told properly.

The opinions expressed, and all errors, are mine.

Part One

Towards the solution

I start by outlining the question which this book tackles – how to schedule our advertising, mainly in television.

The second chapter describes some results of media research which indicate how many people are given the opportunity to see the advertising. This is the basis for forecasting and is combined with the amount advertisers expect to pay to have their ads transmitted.

In Chapter 3, I describe how the advertiser specifies the times of year he would prefer to influence shoppers.

To these two descriptions of the environment for the schedule I could have added competitors' activities. Especially for small advertisers, ducking under the competition could be important. If you believe it is share of voice that influences sales most, this could be a smart policy.

I have not discussed this in detail, though it appears in the notes on Chapter 1 and can influence our decisions about the values of different times of the year. It is not a factor considered by many advertisers, maybe because the forecasting involved is uncertain. Some analysts find the effect of competitors' advertising hard to measure, either because it is a rather contin-uous background, or because en masse it has little specific effect and it is particular advertisers we should look out for.

Costs and values are the relatively easy part of the work. The complications start when we try to specify the effects we expect, based on how we understand the past. It is here that most of the disputes take place. It is tempting – and traditional – to try to schedule without paying much attention to the detail of advertising effects. This is fatal, because 'how advertising affects sales' itself affects how we should schedule. My own view is expressed in Chapters 4 to 6, and competing theories are in Part 2.

Because some of the factors will differ across campaigns, advertisers do not all compete for the same solution. Media can accommodate clients with different needs.

Chapter 6 is different. It is about the conventional analyses of how our TV campaign was 'seen' by the industry's viewing panel. I explain why this separate view of our schedule, based on an analysis of individuals, is necessary. It complements our real priority – to maximise sales-effectiveness.

Putting together what you have to pay, when you most want to have an effect, and how you believe the advertising will work – that is the central problem. From the way I define the mechanics, a solution can be reached. This is described in Chapter 7.

This uses the 'CV-DD' model: shorthand for
- **C**osts, or what you have to pay for TV time each week,
- **V**alues, or what it is worth to you to apply advertising pressure each week to the relevant shoppers,
- **D**ecay in the effects of advertising, and the rate of
- **D**iminishing returns.

I believe these factors, plus of course the budget and some housekeeping details, determine how we should lay down our money. Leaving out any one of them – as some have suggested – maims the solution, for each of them plays an essential part. That is why Chapters 2 to 5 explain these terms and how to estimate their contribution.

I start by asking the planner to describe the brand's situation. It hardly needs to be said that this varies from one campaign to another.

My recommendation is then very different from general advice, such as 'Three exposures in a short time interval are needed for advertising to be effective', or, 'Be continuous'. Such suggestions cannot be appropriate to every situation. Instead, I suggest a *process* which takes into account the planner's information, objectives and guidance.

The process may sound complex when the technical details are spelled out. In practice, these are not the concern of users, who have only to describe their situation, needs and resources in terms they are familiar with.

As well as allocating the budget over time, we sometimes have to allocate it across regions. The two sorts of decision interact, so are better thought of together. In Chapter 8, I discuss this briefly.

I am under no delusion that this is the last word in scheduling. I hope the industry will improve and agree on its understanding of how advertising can work over time, under different circumstances and with a variety of objectives. Knowing this better, we will also make more effective decisions about when to advertise. It is my wish only to contribute to this improvement.

Thus Part 1 proposes a way to solve the problem, to construct a schedule which achieves the best results. My own opinion on these matters has led to the process I put forward.

But this depends on beliefs about campaign effects which are not shared by everyone. The subject is controversial. I am well aware that there are competing methods. Different researchers have suggested various strategies, based on their own views of how advertising works, how the effects should be measured and how these measures should be interpreted. I acknowledge that some have very valid claims.

Hence I show in Part 2 how my position compares with others. Their views, and the basis for them, are described there. There are still many parts of this problem where we have too little shared information. On some, we are all ignorant. The reader will have to choose between conflicting theories.

In order to bring the subject to life, and to describe how it is possible that we disagree, I also paint some of the background against which the alternatives developed, and I sketch in some of the people who have contributed. This is meant to help the reader to see the subject as it really is – evolving by the insights of individuals, by debate and by competition.

Chapter 9 is about the early work of Colin McDonald and Chapter 10 is about the development of other theories of how advertising works and of their implications.

Chapter 11 describes how the scene was completely changed by John Philip Jones, Walter Reichel and Erwin Ephron. More recently, reactions to these new ideas and work by Andrew Roberts have altered the landscape again and these subjects are discussed in Chapter 11.

1   What is the problem?

The main subject

The problem discussed in most of this book is how to allocate an advertising budget over a period of time. A schedule written using the ideas set out here may save hundreds of thousands of pounds.

Usually the campaign plan is for one year or less; a year is the time planned here. The unit of time may be a month, a week or a day; a week is the period assumed in most of the book. The problem arises with all media, but has received most research attention for television; thus television language is generally used. The main application is: how to write an efficient TV plan. The solution applies to all media.

Until the mid-1990s, most large advertisers concentrated their television advertising. Setting an 'effective frequency' determined how many weeks they could be on air.

The result might be two or three weeks on, followed by two or three weeks off. Like a bird's rapid spurt, followed by a plunge, this is known as 'flighting'. Or, advertising may appear between long intervals and one, two or three times a year. These are 'bursts'.

The notion that there exists a universal effective frequency dominated TV research for decades. To me, it sounds rather like the attempts of governments to control their economies through a single instrument – interest rates. That is to ignore taxes, government spending, manufacture, foreign trade, etc. Effective frequency similarly ignores the brand's situation and objectives, its budget, the copy, the values and costs of different weeks and so on.

Another possibility, sometimes recommended, is to be on air, even at a low weight, nearly all the time. In this way advertising drips steadily into the viewer's head. 'Continuous cover' is then the cry, and frequency is disregarded. This can be modified in several ways. One is to set a minimum rating level, which is connected with cover as we see later.

Of these three extreme shapes of schedule, is one right for your situation? Flights, bursts – or continuity? It sometimes appears that is what we have to decide. Or, is there some other shape, which is best for you?

So 'when' in the title means exactly what it says: a decision has to be made about the *time* when the advertisements are to appear. The title does not mean, 'Whether to advertise or not'. A decision about the budget has already been made (and I have written about it in another book[1]). All that has to be determined now is the schedule: the list of TV ratings (or insertions in other media) to be bought; or, a list of how much money is to be spent in each week (or other period of time).

I say, '*all* that has to be determined'. Indeed, this is a less important decision than, for example, how much to spend or what to say in the ads themselves. We are discussing here an improvement in efficiency of a few per cent. This is not to be neglected. 'A few per cent' of your budget can be well worth adding.

So this is a book about increasing the sales-effectiveness of TV advertising. It rests on the belief that we should first define, and measure, if we can, how TV advertising has benefited the brand. Then, we use this information to write the most effective and relevant schedule. I recommend a common *process*, but an individual *solution*.

Other subjects

The book is a discussion about how TV advertising works. Not in the sense of what goes on in shoppers' heads, but about the measurement of advertising effects and the interpretation of these measurements.

You cannot write an efficient schedule without views about the decay of short-term effects, about diminishing returns, about long-term effects. And you cannot form such views without understanding the research studies put forward as guidance.

This explains why Part 2 of this book is there. The subjects just mentioned are difficult and controversial. Incompatible recommendations have been made with apparent authority. What is the planner to do?

Part 1 of this book is one of several systems put forward. You may simply accept advice, and this is what most people do. But if you want to know about other ideas, and to read about how they came into being, Part 2 reviews the subject for you. It is written as a history, tracing a wandering line of research and speculation from the 1950s to today. I believe that history helps you to make up your own mind. Whatever emerges over the next few years will be a consensus and probably appears in these pages.

The politics of media decisions

The book also describes a clash between competing systems. It is tempting, but over-simple, to say that these competing systems are planning and buying; although it often looks like this.

Most managers see advertising as a marketing tool, which should pay its way. Scheduling is part of the media operation which, just like budgeting, copy development and choice of medium and channel, is judged solely by return on investment. This is my own criterion, and it is the outlook of a good media planner. Sales effectiveness is the judge of which decision is best.

There are also media controllers; managers who make choices between media buying operations and media strategies, who have other criteria. They use media-buying reports, not sales figures, in their definition of 'best'. It is the TV viewing panel they study, not the goods leaving the factory, the retail audit or the consumer panel.

Buyers strive to satisfy both these masters, and their different criteria, for obvious reasons. 'Sales effectiveness' is rarely mentioned by media controllers, and when it is raised as a reason for day-to-day decisions the attempt is seldom convincing.

I do not imply that the job of the media controller is unnecessary, still less that the buyer is unimportant. On the contrary, as the person who has to execute the plan – and who should play a large part in writing it – the buyer's input is vital. Detailed knowledge of the channels, their programming, what sort of viewing goes on at different times of day, the media research available – all this is indispensable. In addition, the buyer has the front-line task of negotiating with the channel owners.

The debate between sales effectiveness and buying 'efficiency' is discussed in the book.

Is timing in the media plan a difficult decision?

For many, scheduling looks like a minor stage in media planning – and even less important in the whole campaign process. It seems to be a tactical and unimportant step, like putting a stamp on an envelope. On the contrary, it is really a strategic decision, which requires you to think through a major question – how will this campaign affect shoppers' behaviour?

For most campaigns, both large and small, the allocation decision is *not* easy. The planner simply does not know how to become more efficient. He is unaware of the cost-savings possible by making a better allocation, or the improvements that can be made in the sales-effectiveness of the schedule. These gains can be out of all proportion to the effort involved.

There are other campaigns for which the scheduling decision is so obvious that little thought is required. A car manufacturer decides to launch a new range at the Motor Show: he therefore advertises just before the show opens. Or, my brand is allocated a focus period of promotions: I therefore announce these with advertising at the same time. The pattern is clear enough.

I have just said that the gains can be much larger than the costs of taking the trouble to schedule well. Yet the decisions are often made with little thought. Simplicity and rules of thumb are favoured above effectiveness. Why is this?

The first reason is simply tradition: this is how decisions have been made for decades. The second reason is that, without relevant competition between schedulers there is no incentive to change. There is competition, of course, but it is still largely on cost within certain rough restrictions. The media department and the media independent are not rewarded in proportion to the sales made.

More understandably, the basis for the improvements are not exact: most advertisers do not know how their campaigns are going to work. Again, buys cannot be precisely forecast, so calculations of benefit have to be rough. In my view, these are not sufficient excuses for inaction.

Examples

By looking at some actual schedules, we see the issues more clearly. Four examples are now given, two for the supermarket chain Sainsbury's and two for Unilever brands. The region chosen is real,[2] but is called here 'Northland', so that the findings do not sound local. The year is 1997 and the only channel studied for the first example is the largest TV station in the region.

These are typical 'as-bought' schedules. In practice we never see the tidy bar charts shown in plans, and for good reasons. Audiences are not so predictable, and the negotiation of buys is not determined by neatness.

In the autumn, Sainsbury's ran a promotion with British Airways, and advertised it for two weeks only – obviously tied to the timing of the promotion. The schedule is in Figure 1.1.

Advertising for Sainsbury's fresh food ran in the seasonal peak, May to July: see Figure 1.2. There was probably more flexibility for the timing of this advertising.

Unilever advertised its Persil Wash-up Liquid in three bursts – February–March, April–May and September. These are shown in Figure 1.3.

But for the more heavily advertised Surf detergent, advertising was on nearly all year, though there were still several clear gaps. For the example in Figure 1.4, data were recorded for all the channels used to ensure that these gaps were deliberate.

These four figures make it clear that schedules can have different shapes. But, to anticipate an obvious comment, more is going on than just the size of the budget.

Where the purpose is clearly limited, or the budget is small, we expect to see advertising limited to a few weeks, though even then, these weeks might be chosen in a variety of ways. In other cases, market seasonality is not

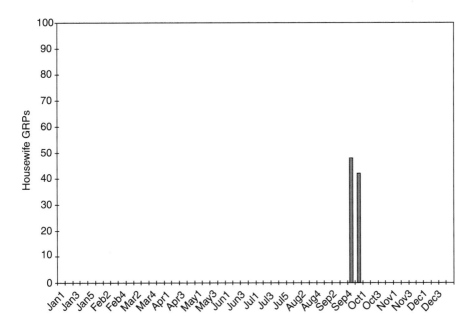

Figure 1.1 Schedule for Sainsbury's BA promotion, Northland 1997
90 ratings total on main commercial channel

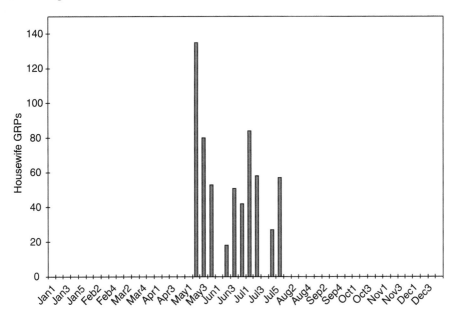

Figure 1.2 Schedule for Sainsbury's Fresh Food, Northland 1997
605 ratings total on main commercial channel

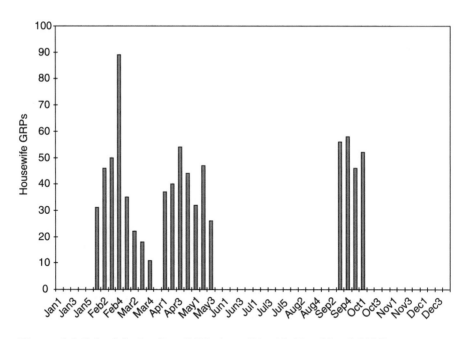

Figure 1.3 Schedule for Persil Wash-up Liquid, Northland 1997
794 ratings on main commercial channel

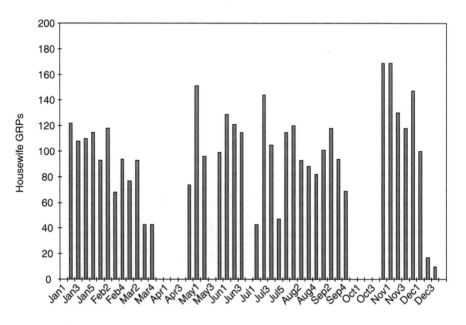

Figure 1.4 Schedule for Surf, Northland 1997
3,948 ratings on all channels

strong and the decision about timing must be subject to different influences. How much attention is the scheduler paying to audience size and cost considerations? How much does he believe in a better effect from concentrating the effort? These are questions examined in later chapters.

A more general review of UK scheduling has been carried out by TSMS[3] and shows the propensity to burst. Of 113 schedules analysed, for advertisers using the tvSPAN service, the percentage of brands following each pattern is given below; also, the percentage of total housewife impacts.

	% by brand	% by impacts	Weekly rate when on
Flight	8	8	83
Burst	64	50	102
Continuous or drip	23	38	63

It makes no real difference in which country such decisions are being made. In the US, costs are about average by global standards. In the UK, TV costs are relatively high, and budgets for most brands are relatively small. Thus, British planners have to be more cautious in spreading their small hoard of precious ratings. In some Asian countries, the number of ratings which can be afforded is higher, but this does not mean that when they should appear is a trivial decision.

Part of a bigger process

The decision about spreading the TV budget over the year is not made in isolation. It is part of a process which includes business planning, marketing and communication decisions and the creation of advertising. I do not provide the detail of this bigger picture, but a checklist for the relevant parts of the media briefing is given in the notes.[4]

Although print and other media are mentioned, this is a book about TV scheduling. The principles apply to other media, but the language, data and attitudes differ. I do not mean by this that other media do not matter, or that they should be planned separately – it is important to integrate other media with TV when they are used.

The following information, which we need in this book, has been determined by the team:
– The budget for airtime.
– The time the campaign is to cover, and how this is broken up into reporting periods – for example, a calendar year, with buying reports each month.

- The definition of the TV target audience, in terms of which ratings data will be available.
- Creative plans for the campaign, including of course spot lengths and anything which affects choice of dayparts, programmes and so on.
- Information about the category and the brand situation, which will help us make technical decisions later.
- Any special restrictions or deals which limit or otherwise affect the choice of channels and dayparts.
- Information from analyses of the performance of earlier campaigns, for this or related brands, which will assist scheduling.
- Other marketing activities supporting the brand, especially those with which TV is to be associated, such as promotions and other media.
- Other brands or umbrella advertising from the parent company, whose timing could be relevant to ours.
- The main competitors to the brand, and what is known or estimated about their campaigns.
- If different regions of the country are involved, details which help in allocation of the TV budget across them.
- Plans for experiments and for post-campaign evaluation, which we can use to help with scheduling and other future decisions.

Using history

I have now used the words 'better' and 'improvement'. It is in the exact definition of these words that the solution lies. The story told in this book is also the story of attempts to define and measure what advertising actually achieves. Only in this way can we make best use of it.

The underlying principle is that we first need to understand the past. What have we learned about advertising effects? Then *consistent* thinking is used to evaluate the different schedules we might buy. The plan is based on experience about the return we – and others – have had on the advertising investment.

My own experience has been that adstock modelling is a good way to explain advertising effects on sales. This is briefly described here. It can be applied to the sort of data most advertisers have. Hence, the solution put forward is also an adstock model.

I am aware that simpler solutions are preferred by many. There are planners who want sound-bite scheduling. They see a one-line instruction on how to write a media plan as the ideal. But I believe the situation is complex and calls for a corresponding response. This does not mean the answer is difficult, only that it must be careful and appropriate. All it really needs is for the planner to describe the situation and objectives of the brand and the campaign: the rest is done by computer subject to human quality control. The problem can be solved by a process and that is provided here.

In particular, I contrast my approach with attempts to understand the past by over-simple analyses of OTS contingency tables, using single-source data. This is often combined with criteria for schedule analyses of OTS distributions, using industry viewing panels. I explain in Part 2 why I believe this approach can be flawed.

I do not go into great detail about the decision to allocate money over different regions, when a country has a TV network which makes this possible. But this does influence the scheduling decision, so it is summarised in Chapter 8.

She or he

Many media planners, buyers and researchers are women. So are many advertisers, managers and sellers of media time and space. I hope they will accept that I understand this very well, having worked for and with many of them. It is only to keep the text flowing, when talking about professionals, that I write 'he' and not the clumsy 'she or he'. The majority of housewives, or homemakers as they are known in the US, are still women.

2   What do you pay for different times?

Introduction

The unit for scheduling TV time is usually a week, though four weeks and months are often used, and so are days. The question discussed in this chapter is, what will you have to pay each week?

The details, of course, depend on decisions made by the brand team, particularly spot length, channel and daypart; also, when relevant, which regions are to be used. The answer, once he has all the information needed, is supplied by the buyer. What I describe here is the broader picture, the seasonality of TV costs.

Forecasting this seasonality is one of the easier jobs to be done before scheduling. It is vital, not only for this purpose, but because buyers are compared ruthlessly, after the event, on the price they paid. The comparison is made with their own forecasts, as well as with their competitors. Hence the subject is well researched.

Our objective is simpler than the buyers'. We need to know how total costs will vary across the year. They have to compare different channels and different dayparts, not just the overall cost. They deal with the detail, we are often content with monthly and sometimes with quarterly figures. They continually adjust their estimates in the light of performance, we are usually writing a one-off annual plan.

Seasonality in other media does not get the same attention. In print, for example, the nominal cost of advertising often does not vary through the year. This is because, unlike television, a newspaper or magazine can alter its inventory by adding pages. The effect is not so different, if you believe that in a thicker publication your advertisement gets less attention, but this is seldom allowed for.

Setting the scene

Media buying is a negotiation in most countries. The seller has a ratecard, but knows he is in competition with other media, and is often ready to do a deal. Sometimes he sticks to the published costs, but nowadays this is an exception.

Whether or not a specific deal is struck, prices are ultimately determined by the market. In the next chapter we see seasonality from the advertiser's point of view in detail – here we are concerned with its effect on overall demand.

The buyer for a particular campaign knows how special circumstances modify the average in his case. There will be effects from the importance of the advertiser to the media owner, the budget size, the time the order is placed and so on. But in general, the way costs vary over the year is the same for all advertisers.

The definition of the target audience is crucial. The transmissions cover some defined geographical region. We know the details of the universe in this region – how many homemakers or housewives can receive the signal, for example (these are the people solely or mainly responsible for household duties; they may be male or female).

Definitions

Within this universe, and for each commercial spot transmitted, research is available to estimate the audience to the spot. The exact definition of 'being exposed' to advertising varies with the research method used and also does not concern us. The point is that each member of a research panel is classified as either having an *opportunity to see* the spot or not. This definition, abbreviated to OTS, is the unit in everything which follows.

Another word used is 'impact', which means that a person in a particular target audience has an opportunity to see. The number of people in the potential audience, times the rating of a spot (divided by 100), is the number of impacts the spot has achieved. In other words, we have bought this number of opportunities the target audience has to see.

'Time shifting' might complicate the story. A video recording, made in the home from a live programme, may be played back soon after or much later (or not at all!). Some viewing of commercials takes place later than the time of transmission. I view these OTS as a bonus and do not count them in what follows.

Ratings can be added for all the spots in the campaign for any period. This gives its total rating points, called GRPs or Gross Rating Points in most of the world, TVRs or Television Rating Points in the UK, TARPS or Television Audience Rating Points in Australia and New Zealand. The names all mean the same and I stick to ratings or GRPs from now on.

Cost per rating point is a unit used for describing how costs vary – over different target audiences, different times of year, different regions and countries. Cost for one hundred rating points is also often used. One hundred GRPs means that, on average, every member of the target has had one OTS. However, you must appreciate that with one hundred ratings many people are not covered (have no OTS), and some have more than one. Another unit is cost per thousand, meaning that this amount of money (dollars, pounds and so on) buys a thousand impacts.

The first two units vary by size of region – larger potential audiences mean more viewers per rating point. The third unit is independent of region size.

Supply and demand

Costs are determined, as usual, by supply and demand.

The supply of TV time is assessed by the advertiser in two main stages. First, how *important* is the universe offered – for example, how many housewives can receive the station signal, and how valuable are these particular housewives? Second, what *percentage* of this universe are likely to see the commercials? This means the ratings (or impacts), which are estimated from historic data, with common-sense adjustments.

The adjustments depend mainly on the attraction of the programme schedule, plus a view on the ability of other stations or other leisure pursuits to seduce away the historic audience. There are usually small or predictable variations round a seasonal pattern which is very regular. There are famous exceptions, like the failure to forecast the impact of the World Cup on ratings in the UK in 1998.

'Demand' is the pressure put on the sellers of TV time by advertisers in total, in their need to be on air.

These two factors vary over the year and in ways specific to the channel, the country or region and its economic health.

Variations in viewing

Examples are the only way to describe these movements, and so I turn to two regions I call Northland and Southshire.[1] Suppose it is the homemakers, or housewives, in these regions who are the target audience. There are 1,500,000 of them in Northland and 721,000 in Southshire, who can be reached by the main commercial TV service in these regions. For simplicity, I ignore the many other TV channels available.

I start with the actual number of OTS for the average homemaker, or impacts, achieved each week in each region. This is plotted in Figure 2.1. It varies mainly with the amount of viewing of the channel, and partly with the number of spots sold by the station. The latter does not vary much, since the channel tries to sell all its commercial minutes.

The pattern of viewing is similar in both regions, but there is more viewing in Northland. Each week, on average, a homemaker there saw 167 commercials from this channel; in Southshire, only 137. These averages are 24 and 20 a day. The amount of viewing alters with the programmes offered, and with the attraction of other channels, but mostly with the total time spent in front of the TV set. This clearly dips in the summer in a very regular way.

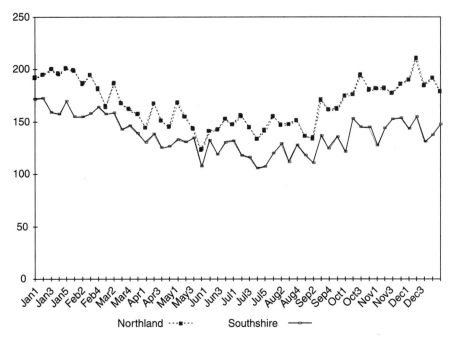

Figure 2.1 Housewife OTS per week

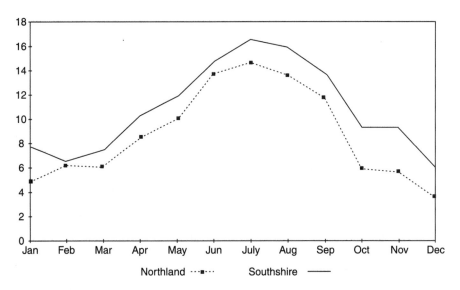

Figure 2.2 Average temperatures (°C)

20

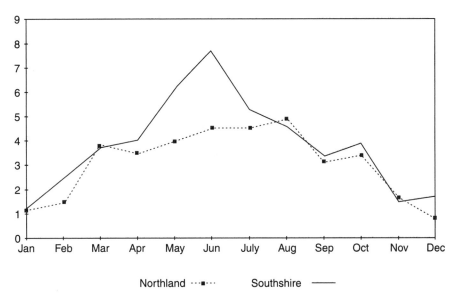

Figure 2.3 Hours of sun

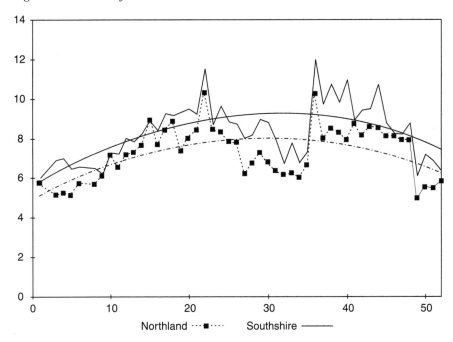

Figure 2.4 Costs, pounds per 1,000 housewives OTS, 1997 (with seasonal fits)

The reasons for this are obvious. As we move towards warmer evenings and more daylight, viewing drops. During September and October, homes settle into their winter pattern. Figures 2.2 and 2.3 show the patterns in temperature and in hours of sunshine – both of which are higher in Southshire. People watch more television when it gets cold and dark; programme schedulers accentuate this by launching their autumn schedules.

Variations in costs

But costs do not follow the viewing patterns exactly in reverse. That is, high viewing does not automatically mean low cost and vice versa. Figure 2.4 is not simply the mirror image of Figure 2.1. The reason is the variation in demand.

To investigate this, we need the revenue of the TV stations. The services which provide the revenue estimates average over a month, or over a quarter in the US. This gives the false impression that actual revenue arrives at a steady rate over these intervals. Hence, costs seem to step sharply up and down by months. This is even more so when costs themselves are estimated, which is normal practice, rather than a revenue estimate being applied to weekly ratings estimates. Even when that is done, as in Figure 2.4, there are some clear jumps.

These steps are artefacts of the way the forecast is constructed. Actual costs, week by week, move more smoothly. But the steps are critical in scheduling. When this is done manually, and by months, we see their obvious effect. Even when it is done weekly, and by an optimising method (as explained in Chapter 7), the effect is still clear. For example, the method may favour the last week of four, to take advantage of a low cost there before a step up. This may be an artificial gain, but I see no way to change general practice to a more realistic forecast. In any case, uncertainties in viewing data and in controlling buys make it pointless to be too fastidious.

In 1997, Southshire took about £42 million, and Northland £93 million. Dividing the revenue by the number of homemaker impacts in thousands (5.1 million in Southshire and 13 million in Northland) we get the cost[2] of a thousand impacts: £8.70 and £7.10 respectively. In Chapter 8 I show the implications of the fact that Southshire is dearer in this comparison. This is because advertisers are less keen to buy impacts in Northland. There are relatively more households there in the lowest social grade or DEs, 41 per cent compared with 29 per cent in Southshire, so it is less attractive to many advertisers.

When we calculate cost in pounds per rating point, for Southshire this is about £58 and for Northland £107. On this basis Southshire costs less, because its much smaller size outweighs its slightly higher cost per thousand.

There are differences in cost by audience definition, of course, but they all have the same seasonal variation. A homemaker watches more TV than the average adult but the shape is similar. Because the price paid for a spot is independent of the particular audience the advertiser wants to reach, the cost for adults is lower than for housewives (more adults are watching than housewives).

It is the combination of viewing seasonality and the seasonality of advertiser demand which drives the costs of television.

It is possible to estimate the seasonality of this demand. To do so, I use the ratings as an explainer[3] of the variation in costs, and find that they can only be used to explain half the variation. What is left, after this fit, averaged over months in Figure 2.5, estimates the effects of demand. Changes in advertiser pressure reduce costs by between £1 and £1.50 in July and August, and add between £1 and £2 per thousand in the autumn.

The reasons for changes in demand are not hard to describe. Some of them are myths about shoppers, some are dictated by marketing calendars.

There is a tradition of talking to most shoppers after they have emerged from winter hibernation in March, and are thought to be ready to shop in April and May. So costs due to advertiser demand have risen 70 per cent by May, though viewing has fallen by only a quarter.

It is commonly believed by marketers, against the evidence, that 'no one watches TV in the summer', when they are on holiday. July and August are slack months (advertisers go on holiday too!). From June to August the decline in viewing is actually small, but costs have fallen 20 per cent.

The return from holidays in September is seen as a great opportunity, and costs leap up immediately. In December, apart from the makers of toys, perfumes and other gifts, many manufacturers believe it is impolite and probably counter-productive to continue normal advertising (and many have had their annual budgets cut by then anyway).

Changes from year to year

We have now seen similarities in the pattern of viewing across two different regions. The average cost varies from year to year – usually upwards – but the relative week-by-week costs change little, because they are caused by deep underlying trends. Figure 2.6 shows how the pattern was repeated in Northland for 1994 to 1997, while the annual average moved from £5.53, through £6.25 and £6.96 to £7.70 per thousand housewife impacts.

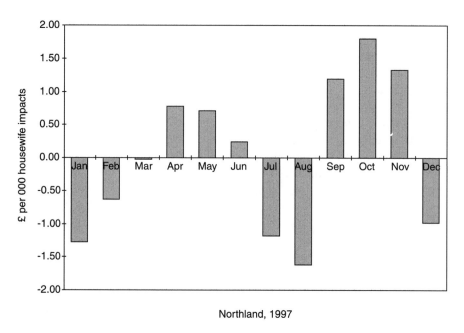

Northland, 1997

Figure 2.5 Seasonality of advertiser demand

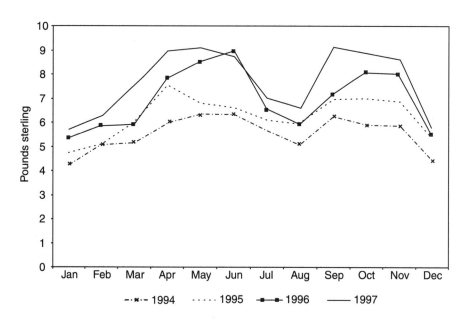

Figure 2.6 Northland, cost for 1,000 housewife impacts

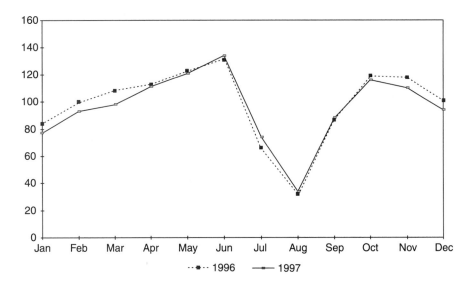

Figure 2.7 Italy: housewife impacts from RAI

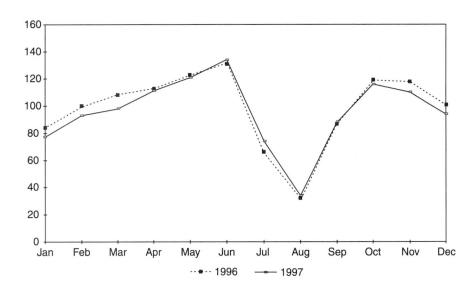

Figure 2.8 Italy: RAI costs per housewife GRP

Are countries different?

Similar work is regularly done in all countries with commercial television. We expect variations across countries, not only because of the reversal of the seasons from south to north of the equator, but because of differences in society, in the economies and in TV practice.

An example is given in Figures 2.7 and 2.8, for the main TV station in Italy, which might have been drawn from any southern European country. North America produces plots similar to Figures 2.1, 2.6, 2.7 and 2.8.

We do not see the same in Australia. Viewing south of the equator is the opposite to Figures 2.1 and 2.7, just as the seasons are. The colder cities, further south, again have higher viewing. Figure 2.9 shows ratings[4] in Adelaide and Melbourne (relatively colder and with longer nights) and in Sydney, Brisbane and Perth. December viewing is quite different from the European Christmas, or from the geographically equivalent June. This is the big social season in Australia, when people are out and about – also programming quality is low then. The week of Christmas and New Year is the big exception, and is not due to peak ratings being up, but off-peak (to cover cricket matches) which raises the average.

Figure 2.9 Grocery buyer TARPS, 1997, Australia

Other media

Research on audiences and revenues for other media is less detailed than for TV. It is usually necessary to rely more on the media researcher's and buyer's interpretation of a variety of data.

Radio is the medium most like TV, in that each member of the audience can have an opportunity to hear each spot. We assume again that each spot was heard only when it was transmitted.

Outdoor advertising can also be seen only when it is posted. *Direct mail* is opened, if at all, when it is received.

Advertising in *newspapers*, and more so in *magazines*, may have a longer life than in the publication period. Later readers may have a copy passed on to them, and read it less thoroughly than early readers, but it can be worth taking such exposure to advertising into account. Thus you can pay for an insertion in January, but some readers are not affected until February. This could be dealt with as part of the decay of effects, but strictly that starts only once an ad has been seen, hence it is mentioned here.

This is particularly so for some types of magazines, which follows from an investigation by Millward Brown[5] in the UK in 1990. More recently, pilot work in the US has been reported.[6]

By showing women reproductions of front covers, Millward Brown established which past issues they claimed to have seen, and hence for how long, after the publication date, reading occasions were still accumulating. Four groups of publications are shown below (there were others).

	Examples
Fat quality monthlies	Vogue, Harpers and Queen
Women's weeklies	Woman, Woman's Realm
Listings	TV Times, Radio Times
Sunday supplements	Sunday, Telegraph Weekend

For the first group, build-up is very slow. Only a quarter of total reading occurs in the month of issue. After two months, it is still only half the total reading occasions that has accumulated; after five months, the figure is still only 80 per cent.

The delay gets less as we move down these groups, until for Sunday Supplements 60 per cent of reading occasions took place within the first week, and most of this is probably on Sunday and Monday.

Interviews with men have shown similar patterns for publications which interest them.

This information on the delay in readership accumulation has been built into schedule analyses. Average issue readership is allocated according to the accumulation curve, followed by the calculation of reach and frequency. For example, Telmar TimePlan analyses generate weekly frequency distributions of exposure to any given press schedule.

Unlike the conventional distributions, it is not enough to know how many saw an ad once in a particular week. We need to know how many saw it for the first time, how many for the second time and so on. Then the system allows a response function (and a wear-out estimate) to be included in the evaluation.

Conclusion

The net of this review is that, for most media, we have a good idea of when advertising is seen, compared with when we place it.

There is great regularity in the way media are used overall. Despite difficulties in forecasting the detail precisely, buyers and planners have reasonable estimates on how overall costs will vary over the coming year.

3 When are the good times to reach people?

Introduction

We want to say *these* weeks are *this* much more important to us than *those* weeks. This is also a relatively easy decision. Knowing what the advertising is *for*, you should find it straightforward to put a value on the different weeks of the year.

Sometimes it is very easy indeed – for example, when advertising is making an announcement. You then know exactly when you want people to be aware of what you have to say. Even in other cases, weeks differ in their value to the advertiser.

There should then be a stage at which value and cost are compared. Value is defined here. At the end of the chapter, value and cost, as defined in Chapter 2, are combined.

Defining 'good times'

An essential step in planning a campaign is to decide what the advertising is to *do*. It is from this that we answer the question posed in this chapter.

Here a 'good time' does not mean the most economic time – cost will enter later. The question is, how much does the advertiser want to influence people at a specific time? It is about the value of different times to the advertiser, taking into account only how people might react.

The announcement example has already been given. Similarly, suppose the advertising task is to support the launch of a new brand. This means that the middlemen who are to distribute and sell to shoppers have to be reassured that when the brand is first on sale the potential customers know about its advantages and are eager to try it. Advertising has to explain that the new brand is available, why a shopper should try it, and encourage trial.

It follows that the launch date is vital to the timing. Trade press advertising precedes the launch, so may teasers. If TV is used as the main medium then the main campaign must start when the brand is first on the shelves. In the critical first few weeks, the brand must receive most of the support. Whether or not the brand continues to exist will depend on its initial success; everything must be done to guarantee this.

There are other clear reasons to concentrate on special times. This may mean we use them exclusively, or that we upweight then. Announcing a promotion is the most common example, followed by the launch of new advertising.

For these reasons, there are often 'obligatory' ratings. Before further budget spending takes place, we know in advance that advertising must cover particular periods. Any method of schedule construction must allow for such ratings.

It is less common that advertising fills in the gaps left by other marketing activities. Advertising for established brands works best short term when it says something new. Advertising a promotion is a novelty, and the two often show synergy. Hence, in drawing up the schedule, you must take note of the promotion plan.

Sometimes, in a multibrand company, the plan for the year lays down particular weeks when the marketing effort focuses on our brand. The purposes are, first, to avoid competing with ourselves, and second, that the parent company should be on air, in some form, for as much of the year as possible.

If we are a small brand, and know when our competitors are likely to advertise, we may prefer times when we expect them to be at a low weight or off air.

All of these examples are about the *weeks* we may strongly prefer to advertise. The detail can get down to particular *days*: a preference to advertise close to the main shopping days of the week. Sometimes the *time of day* is important, not just because our target audience is likely to be viewing, but because it is specially appropriate to the product. Cereals at breakfast time is an obvious example. Advertising a soft drink on the radio at times when people are thirsty and out of the house is another example. Posters on the way to the supermarket also show that recent and appropriate advertising is valuable.

The general problem

But what if there is no obvious and pressing reason to aim for particular weeks? A helpful step is to examine how many shoppers are actually in the market each week. In other words, the seasonality of sales in the category in which the product competes. Remedies for winter ailments are bought in the winter; many summer holiday decisions are made in late winter, and so on.

For purchases more considered than groceries, it is not the date of the actual sale that matters but *when* the decisions are being thought through. A family holiday, a new car – these can be discussed weeks before the travel company or car dealer gets the order. The mortgage, the new bank account – these are considered before they are negotiated. It is the Christmas gift decision referred to in the last chapter which creates the pressure on TV time in November and early December. The shopper's attitude to relevant information is different at these times.

Cases where the value of all the weeks in the year are completely uniform are so rare that I have never seen one.

Numerical values

Whatever the argument behind the decision, the planner should give a *number* for the value of every week. This looks like overkill when all he has to say is 'One for weeks 14 and 15, zero on other weeks'. But we need a system which always applies, and this is how we choose to deal with the obligatory weeks (another way is to enter unrealistically high costs for the weeks not to be used). Most of the time, there is a range of numbers which varies continuously across the year.

Examples of category seasonality

I now give three examples of category seasonality. They demonstrate that even when you look at a 'stable' category, there is often a seasonal effect to be seen. In the cases shown, there are no larger trends of growth or decay worth considering. In other cases, you will see other shapes. For example, school holidays and not Christmas may be a time for additional sales.

You always have to make a judgement about the points which look odd when you plot historical market data. Are they likely to be recurring exceptions? Or should we fit a simple curve through the middle of the points? Knowledge of the particular category is needed to answer this question. Remember we are using the data to make a forecast for the year we are planning. Look at several years, if you can, before deciding.

The data periods are made up of weeks, four weeks and months (correcting for the number of working weeks in the month). They show peaks either in the summer or in the winter.

The first case shows moderate differences over the year – except for a week each side of Christmas, sales in the highest week are 18 per cent above the lowest. In the second, sales in the highest four weeks are only 9 per cent higher. In the last example, seasonality is so marked you have to wonder whether summer advertising is worthwhile.

Figure 3.1 is about a food staple, for which sales are clearly very low around Christmas – the family shopping is concentrated on other foods. Since there is only one year's data available, the low in weeks 14 and 15 (Easter holidays) and the high from week 37 (end September) may be worth allowing for – or we could follow the fitted curve.[1]

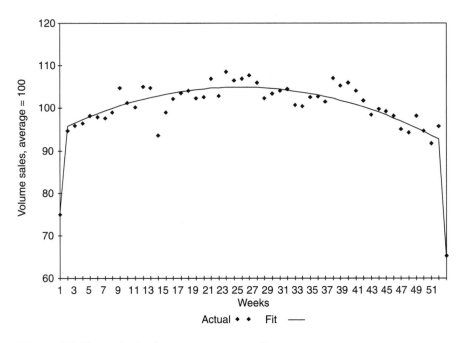

Figure 3.1 Example 1 of category seasonality

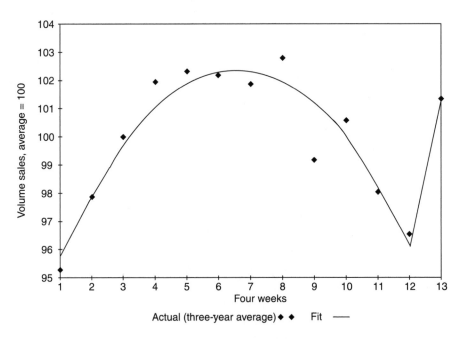

Figure 3.2 Example 2 of category seasonality

There is also a summer high in Figure 3.2, especially in July/August. Unusually for a household product, there is also a high before Christmas – shoppers are both stocking up and using more than in November. Traditionally, this is a 'flat' category, but there is still an explicable seasonal variation worth taking advantage of.

The shape in Figure 3.3 is more extreme and, of course, well known to advertisers of this pharmaceutical product. In fact the surprise is that sales in the summer are not negligible. As sales depend so clearly on the weather, the curve fitted is a good forecast to use.

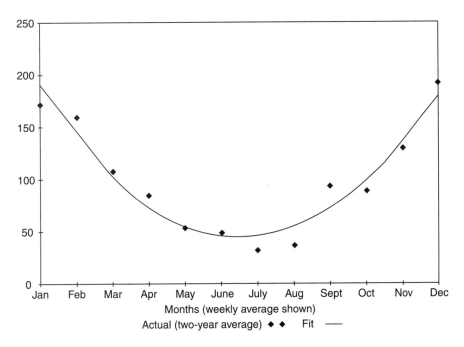

Figure 3.3 Example 3 of category seasonality

Example of brand sales

This example is for a grocery brand in Italy, which chose to use its own sales as the definition of the value of different months. This makes the pattern more variable than when a whole category is used, as in the last three examples. Figure 3.4 shows a small peak at Easter and the highest sales in June. There is another high in December.

*Table 3.1. Data and calculations for Value index, Cost index, Value/Cost –
and the result of adstock modelling evaluation*

	Values		Cost per GRP		Value/Cost	Adstock model
	Input	*Index*	*Input*	*Index*	*Index**	*Index***
Jan 1	71	72	63.8	74	98	114
Jan 2	71	72	63.8	74	98	117
Jan3	71	72	66.0	76	95	116
Jan 4	71	72	66.0	76	95	119
Jan 5	71	72	64.9	75	96	124
Feb 1	77	78	67.1	77	101	124
Feb 2	77	78	67.1	77	101	127
Feb 3	77	78	67.1	77	101	130
Feb 4	77	78	70.4	81	96	128
Mar 1	108	109	75.9	87	125	121
Mar 2	108	109	78.1	90	122	117
Mar 3	108	109	81.4	94	117	112
Mar 4	108	109	84.7	98	112	108
Mar 5	108	109	89.1	103	107	102
Apr1	86	87	92.4	106	82	100
Apr 2	86	87	93.5	108	81	101
Apr 3	86	87	94.6	109	82	103
Apr 4	86	87	95.7	110	79	105
May 1	114	116	96.8	112	104	105
May 2	114	116	97.9	113	102	105
May 3	114	116	102.3	118	98	101
May 4	114	116	123.2	142	81	84
Jun 1	144	146	101.2	117	125	101
Jun 2	144	146	95.7	110	132	104
Jun 3	144	146	93.5	108	135	103
Jun 4	144	146	88.0	101	144	105
Jul 1	108	109	82.5	95	115	109
Jul 2	108	109	82.5	95	115	109
Jul 3	108	109	86.9	100	109	103
Jul 4	108	109	84.7	98	112	105
Jul 5	108	109	78.1	90	122	113
Aug 1	106	107	73.7	85	126	119
Aug 2	106	107	73.7	85	126	118
Aug 3	106	107	73.7	85	126	118
Aug 4	106	107	86.9	100	107	99
Sep 1	117	119	130.9	151	79	65
Sep 2	117	119	105.6	122	97	78

| | Values | | Cost per GRP | | Value/Cost | Adstock model |
	Input	Index	Input	Index	Index*	Index**
Sep 3	117	119	105.6	122	97	75
Sep 4	117	119	102.3	118	101	74
Sep 5	117	119	101.2	117	102	70
Oct 1	75	76	99.0	114	67	70
Oct 2	75	76	99.0	114	67	71
Oct 3	75	76	97.9	113	67	72
Oct 4	75	76	100.1	115	66	72
Nov 1	73	74	101.2	117	63	73
Nov 2	73	74	95.7	110	67	80
Nov 3	73	74	90.2	104	71	89
Nov 4	73	74	90.2	104	71	95
Dec 1	121	123	83.6	96	127	105
Dec 2	121	123	70.4	81	151	113
Dec 3	90	91	68.2	79	116	105
Dec 4	90	91	68.2	79	103	101

* so the average is 100

** see Chapter 5

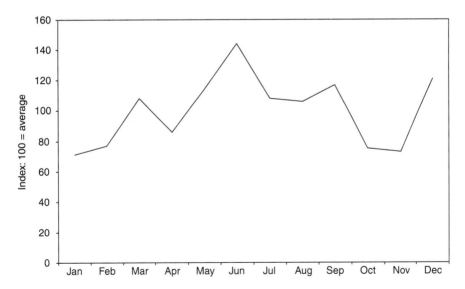

Figure 3.4 Values of months for a grocery product, Italy

Evaluating weeks: Value/Costs

It is now possible to combine the ideas in this chapter with the costs in the last one. Previously, the costs in each week, to reach housewives in Northland and Southshire, were described. I have combined and smoothed these numbers to provide a typical and realistic example of what sort of costs might be estimated for a future plan. The data are given in Table 3.1.

Suppose we also have data which allow us to attach a value to each week. For example, monthly numbers for the rate of category sales. I have attached these to individual weeks, also in Table 3.1.

For both variables, values and costs, I have indexed the weekly numbers so that the average is 100 – since it is only the relative sizes which matter here. Then I divided the Value index by the Cost index.

This is the Value/Cost index – a useful way of providing an overall evaluation of the individual weeks. If this index is high, it is because values are high or costs are low – a good time to invest. If it is low, values are low or costs are high – times we might wish to avoid.

It is implicit in this index that the OTS work very quickly, an assumption which is often close to reality but which is discussed in the next chapter. A correction, if needed, is provided at the end of Chapter 5.

The Value/Cost index is plotted in Figure 3.5. The summer in this case is a good time, because values are high, especially in June, and costs are low, especially in August. October and November are poor months, with very low value and high costs. Again the detail is given in Table 3.1 – but the last column in that table is not explained until Chapter 5.

This example is typical of many campaigns. Some have even sharper value seasonality and hence more variation in Value/Cost. Even when values are flatter, costs still provide marked variation. The actual pattern is, of course, particular to the brand or at least the category and country. This variation from case to case is the most obvious reason why there cannot be a consistent 'best' schedule.

More on the Italian example

Costs in Italy were shown in Figure 2.8. The highs (in May and October) are two-and-a-half-times more expensive than the cheap time in August.

When this is put together with the values in Figure 3.4, which are still high when costs are low, we get Figure 3.6, with massive variation. The summer, and perhaps the month of December, look like the times at which to concentrate advertising. This is investigated in Chapter 7.

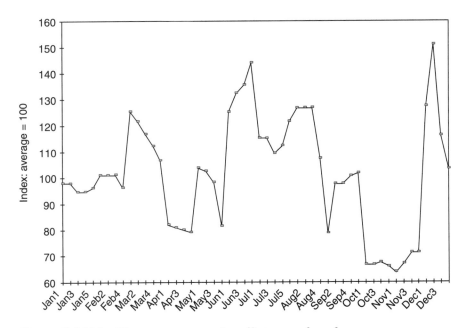

Figure 3.5 Value/Cost to compare the efficiency of weeks

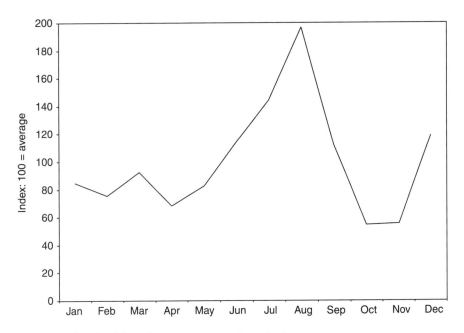

Figure 3.6 Value/Cost for grocery product, Italy

Conclusions

You now have three essential building blocks in scheduling. The *Value/Cost* information sometimes solves the problem on its own as it directs you to the right time.

When we come to evaluate or construct different schedules, we use the information as follows.

You start with a given budget, not a given number of rating points. You have to turn the spend into the 'pressure' on your target at different times (this is defined later). To do this, you have to decide on the ratings you will buy each week. The *costs* you expect to pay each week are necessary for this.

Once you know the pressure on shoppers which your schedule has created in a particular week, you still have to decide how relevant this is for your campaign objectives. That is, how *valuable* it is to have advertising effects at this time.

4   How do advertising effects decay?

Introduction

The next two chapters describe inputs to the scheduling decision which are more contentious than the last two. You can think of them as describing the *sort* of schedule we want, while the last two were about the environment in which the schedule goes to work.

We are now studying the individual campaign, or rather the advertisements that make up this campaign. Paradoxically, we do not concentrate on the advertisements themselves, but on the job for which these ads were written. As Sheridan Morley wrote, 'As a critic, I have spent far too much time watching the stage and not enough looking at the audience.' We are going to look at the audience, at the effects.

Some traces are left in the memory after an opportunity to see an advertisement. The viewer's subsequent contact with the brand advertised can be coloured by parts of the message. The longer after the OTS, the smaller these effects are.

The caution in this description of the effects of seeing an ad is deliberate. There are three reasons.

– First, decay in what? And measured how? When asked, 'What advertisements did you see yesterday?' people are often unable to recall more than two or three. Yet when shown the actual commercials, they know very well that they have seen them. The prompt used, or more generally, the research technique used, makes a big difference to how we answer.

– Second, some readers may have an over-simple view of how advertising may work in their case, and I want to warn them that things may not be so easy.

– Finally, because the situations of the brands advertised and the effectiveness and ways of the advertising working are so varied, any general description is almost impossible. The reservation, 'studying the individual campaign', is essential.

The category in which the brand operates may be of no great interest to the viewer at the time, or it may be a subject of importance. The brand may be well known, the commercial likewise, or the brand may not have made any conscious impression yet on the viewer. The purpose of the commercial may call for immediate action – an appeal for a charity might cause a phone call making a donation. Or, the advertiser hopes for the inclusion of the brand on tomorrow's mental shopping list. Or, the ad may have no 'new news' and be intended mainly to keep the relationship warm between the shopper and the brand. It may be great advertising, attention-grabbing and with proven sales-effectiveness, or it may be boring, ineffective and even a turn-off.

But if the commercial works at all, this means that on some future occasion, feelings and actions will be different. The occasion is usually the need to take some buying decision in the category. There is an 'empty box'; the need to get more breakfast cereal or shampoo or the petrol gauge is close to empty. Or, the occasion may be when the product is used, 'They said it tastes like butter, and it does', or, 'This PC really is fast'. In some circumstances, the occasion is an interview when the viewer is asked about advertising or brands.

The challenge to researchers is to tease out advertising effects from those caused by other factors, which sometimes have larger and clearer effects than advertising. Examples of such factors are: In the supermarket, which brands were on special deals? Was our brand on the shelf at all? Was the feature noted in the product one which you would have thought of yourself?

Tracking data, recall and the short term

The evidence for decay which I find the most convincing is when ad recall is measured in tracking studies on awareness. There are fewer causes of confusion here than in sales modelling; in fact it is seldom necessary to include any explanatory factors other than the exposure of the advertisements. This is in distinction to sales effects, where it is always probable that competitors' activities (and other factors) affect the measures we hope to influence with our advertising. So by looking at awareness effects we see decay in a particularly clear way.

This section is about awareness and recall but this does not imply that these effects of advertising are the main concern of this book – they are not. I want to concentrate on sales effects. But they may tell us *how* sales effects are produced.

Figure 4.1 is an unusual example of a Millward Brown plot, but ideal for my purpose. Ignore for the moment the baseline shown. Each year the same commercial was given about 330 ratings; each year prompted ad awareness rose rapidly, and then fell more slowly. The pattern repeats itself very consistently. The observations are closely fitted by their model.

Figure 4.2 is a more typical example. In the first year there were three bursts of advertising for Campaign A, and in the second there were two for Campaign B; the ratings are indicated again at the foot of the chart.

Millward Brown fit not only an Awareness index (comparable to the coefficient for adstock in a regression model, which is explained later), but also the *base* to which awareness is currently falling. In Figure 4.1 we saw

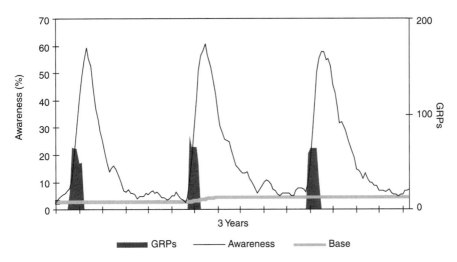

Figure 4.1 Ad awareness for a US brand
(Source: Millward Brown)

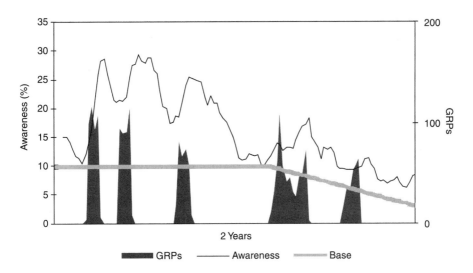

Figure 4.2 Ad awareness for a lager
(Source: Millward Brown)

a slight rise; in Figure 4.2, a fall. In Figure 4.2, we see that during Campaign A the base was at a healthy level, but during Campaign B it goes into decline. Campaign A was able to sustain the base; Campaign B does not hold up the base in the same way.

Such movements in the base demonstrate that advertising can have long-term as well as short-term effects. The sizes of the effects vary with the brand situation and the advertising copy.

In practice, the most important conclusions from Figure 4.2 are that the Awareness index fell with Campaign B (its effect on awareness was only a third that of Campaign A) – and that it did not have good long-term effects either. Obviously there are creative implications, but this is not pursued here.

Adstocks

An alternative to the Millward Brown model[1] is a set of processes known as adstock modelling. A simple adstock model also works well with these examples. I propose that adstock is at the heart of scheduling systems, and I use these examples to explain the process.

Instead of using the schedule of ratings directly to explain ad effects, the schedule is transformed (or pre-modelled, in Tom Corlett's phrase). The decay in its effects is worked out by a formula. Adstock is the calculated current pressure from current and past ratings. I now explain in a non-technical way[2] how this is done.

Some people are put off by the fact that a formula is involved, and that the whole approach needs more than a hand-held calculator. I discuss this sort of difficulty again in Chapter 11. It is a fact of life that if you want an accurate representation of current understanding about ad effects, then you need to use a computer. You can either go into the detail and assure yourself it is sensible, or you can take it on trust and use the aids available. In this respect, scheduling is exactly like most of media planning, from the definition of a television rating onwards.

I return to Figures 4.1 and 4.2 with a different perspective. I use them not only as examples of the fact that these advertising effects decay, I also look at the actual shape of this decay. As in all the examples I have seen, the effect builds while we are on air, and then declines in a gentle curve. This can be represented by a constant rate of decline: while we are off air, and if awareness is x in a particular week, it is dx next week, where d is a decay constant. The week after that, it is d^2x, then d^3x and so on. This is called geometric decay, because the name for 1, d, d^2 and so on is a geometric series.

In order to fit, or model data like Figure 4.1, we have to choose a value of d. It turns out that here it is about 0.92. When modelling other data sets, other values of d are found to fit better. The recommended method is charmingly naïve: just try different values and see which fits best. As so often in this subject, the mantra is, 'Let the data decide'.

One further step is recommended. The parameter d is used by some people as a description of the rate of decay. You might say there is nothing wrong with that. But its meaning does not jump off the page. The result of increasing $d = 0.92$ to $d = 0.96$, for example, is not obvious. But there is another way of defining the rate of decay: the time by which half the total effect has been felt. This is called the half-life of the advertising (strictly, of its effect). The analogy is with radioactive decay.

There is a one-to-one relation between any parameter d and the corresponding half-life and vice versa (another formula is needed to describe it). Half-life is recommended as the description of whether the decay in a particular situation is fast or slow. The half-life corresponding to $d = 0.96$ is about 18 weeks. That is, changing d from 0.92 to 0.96 corresponds to doubling the half-life of the advertising.

Modelling the effects of advertising can be done by using adstock as one of the explainers in a regression on the effect studied. This again is a technical process not described here. The coefficient for adstock tells us how large the effect of advertising is. For this we have to choose a rate of decay, or half-life, in the way described above. This is done here in Figure 4.3,

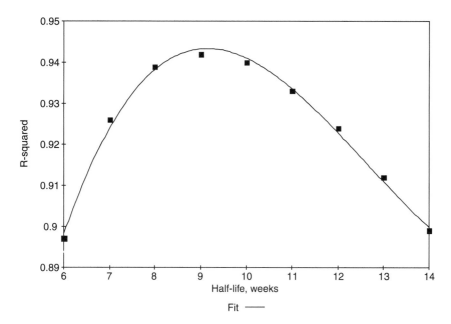

Figure 4.3 What half-life to use? Fits to Millward Brown awareness data using different half-lives

which shows the goodness of fit (R-squared) for several different half-lives. These were used to 'explain' Figure 4.1, and a curve is fitted to these points to emphasise the shape and indicate the optimum. The half-life chosen was nine weeks.

But we have to remember that the tracking score shown is a rolling average for the current and previous three weeks (to smooth out the results) with gaps at Christmas (though the fits by Millward Brown are on actual weekly data). So the 'real' half-life was nearer six weeks than nine. Conventionally, this rate of decay, or for shorter half-lives, is called a 'short-term' effect.

Of course we are doing modelling of this type (but with sales as the objective, not awareness) in order to learn what half-life to use when we come to scheduling.

Long-term sales effects

We can all remember, for the brands we use, some advertising and some slogans that we actually saw more than a year ago. These are examples of 'long-term' effects on memory. Sales can also be influenced by advertising seen long ago.

It is important that the paragraph above includes 'for the brands we use'. The main reason why long-term effects exist is that there is some reinforcement or synergy between experience of the product – whether it be purchase, consumption or just seeing it around – and what the advertising told us about it. A word[3] for this effect is 'framing' – the ad directs attention to a particular feature.

More often than not, the message has got attached to the product; it is part of what we call the 'brand'. Often the mechanism is simply satisfied and repeated purchase. An ad said, 'Why not try this?' You did, you enjoyed the experience, and as a result you continue to buy it. This can be a long-term effect, without the ad *directly* causing the most recent purchase; indeed you have probably forgotten the ad, though it was the cause of a long sequence of decisions.

Another mechanism worth mentioning is that advertising may transform a thing into something resembling a person – and we remember people. Just as primitive societies created wood nymphs and river gods, this anthropomorphism is a powerful hook in the memory.

Colin McDonald put the concept as follows: 'The long-term effect is keeping alive the desirable image which is already in our minds, replenishing the emotional strata laid down by earlier advertising.' That, I agree with. But he also said,[4] and many have thought, 'I can make no sense of the idea of a long-term effect which was qualitatively different from the short term.' On the contrary, I see a need to separate the two and I believe the mechanisms are distinct. I should also repeat that image maintenance and 'emotional strata' are the means by which sales are created and defended, and are not themselves objectives.

I believe that both short-term and long-term effects have their largest impacts immediately after seeing the ad. To say that both *can* exist does not mean both *are* detectable every time.

Later, we meet the claim that there can be no long-term effect without a short-term one. There is no evidence for this which convinces me. I think we can have either or both – or, unfortunately, neither sort of effect is measurable for some campaigns: not all advertising works.

The 'time-bomb' theory has been suggested, but no one I know has ever held it. This proposes that you may not detect any effect at all when the ad is seen, but somehow it affects purchases long after. A malicious tradition attributes this to agencies whose work is actually ineffective. Note, however, that the overall or cumulative long-term effect, when described by adstock, may indeed be much larger than the reaction seen in a day or two. A long-term effect starts immediately – it just goes on longer – but the rate of its effect is still largest at the beginning.

Another idea which can be disregarded is the analogy with data on learning. Experiments on the time for which we retain what we try to learn have been quoted as evidence. But the motivations and conscious processes are quite different and little attention should be paid to such work.

Finally, there may be cases when advertising has effects on the base. These may occasionally be to lift it quickly to a new level. Or, our brand's base may be subject to constant erosion (from competitive activity) but is maintained at a broadly steady, but still varying, level (the so-called floating base model).

For scheduling, the possibilities of a short-term effect and of a long-term effect are sufficient.

What do adstocks look like?

Figure 4.4 shows how a flight or burst of GRPs produces adstock which lasts beyond the end of the burst. Advertising is concentrated in weeks 5 to 8, so the effect starts in week 5. In both cases the area under the curves equals the total in the bars showing the original GRPs – total adstock equals total GRPs.

Two half-lives are used in this figure to demonstrate the result of faster or slower decay. With a short half-life (the full line in the plot), the pressure from advertising rises rapidly. It is at its peak in the last week of advertising, and is virtually all over by ten weeks from the end of the burst; in fact, six

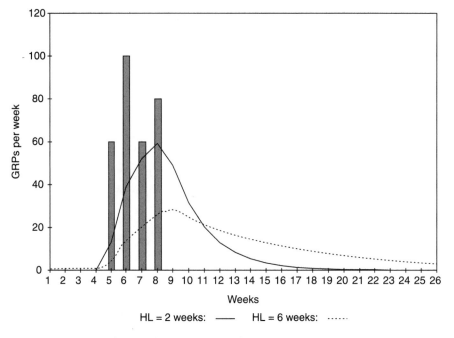

Figure 4.4 Example of adstocks from a flight of 300 GRPs

weeks after, only ten per cent is left. For a very short half-life, like half a week, virtually everything would be over in a couple of weeks after the flight. But with the longer half-life (the dotted line), there is still 22 per cent of the effects to come after week 26.

Adstock modelling – a sales example

In the following example, the brand is a chocolate biscuit sold in groceries, for which I had 80 weeks of retail audit data. Two factors, in addition to advertising, were found to affect the sales share: the brand's price, relative to other brands, and its distribution less out-of-stocks. By varying the half-life used, the fit was found to vary slightly. This is shown in Figure 4.5, where a curve has again been fitted to make the shape clearer. This is a fairly typical relationship. Adstock with any reasonable half-life gives a better fit than the GRPs at the time (equivalent to adstock with zero half-life), but there is not much to choose between half-lives of three to six weeks. Probably four or five would be chosen. Note that this is shorter than for decay in awareness: we must expect the half-life to vary with different criterion variables and in different circumstances.

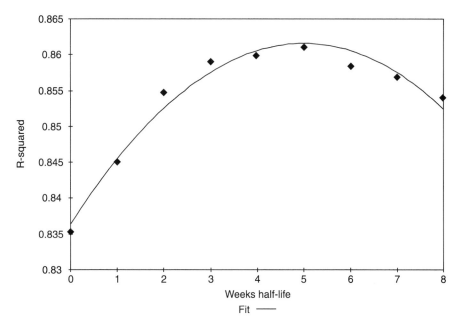

Figure 4.5 What half-life to use? Fits to sales data using different half-lives

With sales data, we are unlikely to get as clear a guide to the appropriate half-life as with awareness scores. In Figure 4.3 the goodness of fit varied considerably as the half-life changed, and the choice of the best fit was clear. This is because no disturbing factors intervened in the effect on awareness. With sales modelling, there is more uncertainty.

The scheduling decisions described in Chapter 7 are equally insensitive, which is to be expected. Exactly because several half-lives would fit real data almost equally well, when we construct a schedule with any of these half-lives we get pretty much the same results. Thus, our main choice will be whether the half-life is very short (a day or two, a half week or one week), rather longer, or genuinely long term. These usually produce very different fits, and as inputs they result in very different schedules.

As examples of long half-lives, I have found 13 and 26 weeks quite often: 52 weeks is the longest I have used. Instead of the sharp variations of short half-life adstock for a burst strategy, there is now a slow-moving curve for the pressure from advertising. Some of these examples have been with data intervals of months or bi-months. The relevance of this comment will be seen in the section below on interval bias. With weekly intervals, over ten or more weeks half-life can count as long term.

Short-term effects are usually easier to detect than long term, but they are often uneconomic. Long-term effects are hard to measure, are often larger than short-term effects, and do pay their way. These facts have misled many analysts, since to justify advertising it is usually necessary to make some attempt, hard and unusual though this is, to estimate the benefits which advertised brands get overall. These are difficult to disentangle from such causes of success as the quality of the product, superior trade relations, price compared with competitors and so on.

Does modelling always give the answer?

We want to know whether to use short-term and/or long-term effects when we come to schedule. For each, we need to use the half-life. In the next chapter we have a similar question about diminishing returns. I recommend we model sales for our brand – or for others like it – to help us decide on the input for scheduling. This does not mean we always get unambiguous and correct answers.

One obvious reason is that we may have a new campaign, or want to emphasise a particular aspect of it – what priority do we give this time to immediate sales, and what to brand building? Or, we may not have modelling results for anything like the situation we are in. Hence we must allow for the input to be settled by judgment, or at least modified by judgment.

Deciding what our advertising is to do is at least as important as the guidance given by modelling. We are usually choosing between a very short half-life (half a week or at most two weeks) – or a compromise – or a long half-life.

There are other reasons why we should not over-rely on modelling. One is that its assumptions may not be close enough to the real situation. In practice, advertising works as only one part of the input to a shopper's brand decision, and in concert with many other factors. If its content is about a price cut, for example, the result will depend on the size of the price reduction, whether it is also signalled in store, and so on. If about a product improvement, the result will depend on the importance of the change, whether the shopper is reminded on the pack, and other factors. What we analyse as a single campaign may contain a variety of appeals, and compete with a number of competitors' activities. All we can expect as the outcome from this turbulence is a rough average, not the exact addition to or multiplication of sales which the model specifies. Imprecision in the rate of decay, noted for Figure 4.5, is to be expected.

Disentangling the two sorts of effect can also be done only approximately. Fitting adstock with a medium half-life (say, three to eight weeks) may well represent the sum of two effects, one with a short and the other with a long half-life. Indeed, it is common to find a single adstock fitted. The half-life is then a compromise between short and long. The length depends on their relative importance, and also on the length of the gaps off air in the data. It is often nearer the short half-life because the size of that effect is more variable.

The Zielske experiment

The questions tackled in this book have long been around. I now re-examine a 40-year-old experiment[5] carried out by the agency Foote, Cone and Belding in Chicago. The titles of the first reports tell it all: 'How frequently should you advertise?' and 'The remembering and forgetting of advertising'.

The case history is an important one for several reasons. First, it concluded that a more continuous schedule was more effective than flighting. A re-analysis[6] by Julian Simon concluded that four-weekly spacing of advertisements over a year caused twice as many total awareness-weeks as placing all the 13 ads in a concentrated schedule. However, if the objective had been to reach a high awareness peak, it was better to concentrate in the first quarter. This would be the case in a launch, when we aim at high sales penetration as soon as possible.

Second, the study has been influential[7] despite its small size and other drawbacks (direct mail only, recall as the only criterion). It has also been controversial.

Third, the data were inaccessible for 20 years; they were originally published only in a smoothed form. This is not the only time in this book we see that innovative and small-scale research, even with access or other problems, can precipitate discussion and sometimes have a large effect on practitioners.

In this section I outline the experiment and discuss its implication on decay, or 'forgetting'. In the next chapter, I use it again, but as an example of diminishing returns.

Two direct-mail schedules were compared. Both sent a series of 13 different ads to respondents picked at random. Later they were telephoned in order to measure proven recall. One schedule was weekly for 13 weeks; the other was four-weekly and so it covered a whole year. The interviews were timed so that in some of them recall was expected to be at a peak, while for others some decay took place after seeing the ads. The average size of a completed sample for any one week was 91. This is small. If 27 informants claimed recall (a typical figure), the estimate of the real proportion who recalled the ad is 30 per cent, the confidence limits are 21 to 39 per cent. Because this is a wide range, and also because the real data indeed show considerable scatter, it is not such a surprise that only smoothed data were originally reported.

There are ten pairs of interviews for which the change in awareness could be due only to decay. For example, at the end of the concentrated schedule, in week 13, recall was 62 per cent. There was no more pressure on this group; further interviews on different individuals at week 17, four weeks later, showed that recall had fallen to 30 per cent.

For each pair, I can estimate the weekly reduction in recall. For example, 30 is about 0.48 of 62. The weekly decay which produces this is that each week's figure is about 0.83 of the previous one, since 0.83 x 0.83 x 0.83 x 0.83 = 0.47.

Averaging the ten estimates available gives an average decay rate of 0.87. From this it is possible to work out the time by which recall is halved on average, which turns out to be five weeks.

A long-term fit

I have found that when a long-term half-life is used (over six, or certainly over ten weeks half-life), there may or may not also be a detectable short-term effect. A published example[8] with both short-term and long-term effects is for a well-established yellow fats brand in a stable category, with very little sales movement. The objects of this advertising are to maintain these sales, especially against lower-priced Own Label products, and to assist the launch of a low-calorie variant. The launch was successful, though to some extent it cannibalised the main brand.

Relative price was the explainer with greatest effect, the distribution of the variant had the least. The half-life chosen was 26 weeks.

A famous long-term effects analysis

Information Resources Inc., or IRI, have reported various analyses[9] of their database of advertising experiments. These experiments were run on IRI's BehaviorScan panels. In markets where cable was the only source of good TV reception, the company set up split panels of shoppers. It was possible to change the commercials viewed in the two halves of the panel, and so to run weight and copy tests. These were evaluated by records of purchases made in scanner-equipped supermarkets, through special payment cards used by the shoppers. Thus the change in brand choices associated with two sorts of campaign showed the change in sales effectiveness of the advertising.

Out of many hundreds of tests, IRI identified 44 which fulfilled very exacting conditions. A test was selected if it ran during Year 1 (between

1982 and 1988), and the result was a significantly positive sales difference. The volume increase of these tests averaged 22 per cent. Over the following two years there was no advertising difference between the two halves of the panel. Any continuation of a positive sales difference could come only from the variable tested during Year 1.

In fact the sales differences did continue. In Year 2, sales were 14 per cent up on average. In Year 3 they were still 7 per cent higher.

These are amazing results. Because of the admirable test design, there can be no doubt we are seeing a genuine long-term advertising effect. It shows that the sales increase, even over a whole year, can be less than half the overall effect: the 14 plus 7 per cent increases are about the same as the 22 per cent during the test year, and there can be little doubt there were small benefits in later years still. To me, the most likely mechanism involved was the one described previously: 'An ad said, 'Why not try this?' You did, you enjoyed the experience, and as a result you continue to buy it'.

Do these figures tell us anything about the rate of decay of the long-term effect, or about the proportions of short-term to long-term benefits? Of course it would be absurd to talk of a proper fit to these three numbers (22, 14 and 7), but it is possible to indicate the order of magnitude of the answers to these questions.

First, even if there are separate short-term effects, Year 2 would be little affected by them and Year 3 not at all. The ratio 7/14, or one half, indicates the long-term rate of decay. We can deduce, directly from this 'one half', a half- life of about a year.

But if there were no short-term effect, the increase in sales in Year 1 could not be as much as 22 per cent. It takes time for the slow effect to build up, and in fact we would expect only an 11 per cent effect in Year 1 – this follows from an adstock model with a one-year half-life, continuous advertising for one year, and resulting in 14 per cent improvement in Year 2.

Hence, there must have been a short-term effect as well, to bring the sales increase up to 22 per cent. A very small amount of the short-term effect from Year 1 spilled over into Year 2. This is illustrated in Figure 4.6.

Overall, only about a quarter of the extra sales came from the short term; this is from 11/(22+14+7). Three-quarters of the total benefit was from the long term. This estimate is completely compatible with evidence from other cases. We can expect, as a general rule, both a short-term effect and a long-term one. The long-term effect is more important.

The meta-analysis from which this example is taken is being repeated, as I write. Some examples of findings have been released.[10] For example, an average half-life of four weeks in the short term, increasing sales on average 4 per cent, with longer-term effects averaging 4 to 8 per cent.

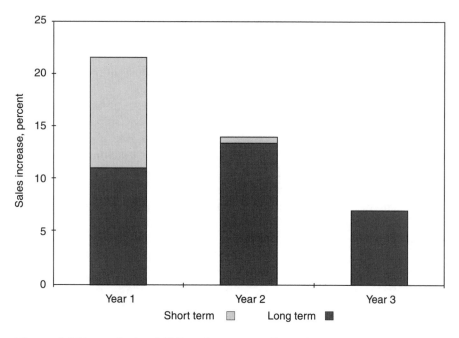

Figure 4.6 Re-analysis of IRI's advertising effects data

Quality of the advertisements

In the fits to data reported above, some readers will miss any reference to the quality of the advertisements. This may mean quality in the sense that the campaign is more or less sales-effective. It is indisputable that there is a vast difference between good and bad campaigns. Or, it may mean differences between executions in the same campaign, though the variety is then usually much less. Or, it may mean differences over time: advertisements 'wear-in' and 'wear-out', or regain their effectiveness after a gap off air.

The first point is easily answered. In fits to data about effectiveness it is usual to include a parameter about the size of this effect. Whether this is small or large is critical to campaign evaluation; it is irrelevant to scheduling. The rate of decay, and the rate of diminishing returns, do however matter; the job of the media planner is to do the best with the advertising he has to plan, whether the effect is going to be moderate or major (improving the advertising is not the subject of this book). Differences between executions are also beyond the control of the media planner.

Effects on the schedule of differences over time[11] can be taken into account, but this is very rare and is not written into this approach. This is because information about wear-in, wear-out and restoration is hardly ever available and is hard to detect in most modelling.

Interval bias

In the first of the examples above, the data were weekly. Shorter intervals – days are ideal – give us a better chance of seeing short-term effects. In the yellow fats example, it was four-weekly. With longer intervals, we are less likely to see short-term effects. More importantly, the longer the data interval, the longer the estimate of half-life, even if real decay is the same. This is for complex statistical reasons explained elsewhere.[12] For long half-lives, this is not a serious concern, but for short half-lives the data interval must be taken into account.

The standard in this book is a single week as the interval for scheduling. The table below indicates the sort of allowance we have to make, if the data analysed to estimate the half-life have different intervals. For example, suppose the original analysis used four-week data and estimated four-and-a-half weeks as the half-life. We should use a three-week half-life in scheduling.

	Interval	
days	*weeks*	*4 weeks*
–	1/2	1.8
0.4	1	2.4
1.4	2	3.4
2.4	3	4.5
3.4	4	5.6
5.3	6	7.7
9.2	10	12.0

Half-life estimated from marketplace data compared with the half-life to use in weekly scheduling. Note that in every case the unit *for half-life is a week*

Conclusions

How should these ideas be used in writing a schedule?

First, we must appreciate that advertisements appearing in one week do not affect sales in only that week, but also for some time after.

How long after? Ideally, this question should be answered by modelling sales for this brand, using various half-lives in measuring decay, and picking the half-life which fits the data best. We should look for both a short-term and a long-term effect, and estimate the size of each.

It is rare that we have the luxury of a fit for our own brand. Next best is to have a library of such fits, and some way of deciding which examples in this collection are closest to our situation, and then use the appropriate half-lives.

If we do not have even this, we need to make a judgment. Do we expect advertising to have a rapid effect? This could be because it is merely a reminder. Or its message – about a promotion, say – is relevant for a very short time. Or, because its intention is to prompt some other immediate action. Then half-lives of a half-week, or as long as a couple of weeks, are appropriate.

At the other extreme, our main purpose may be to 'build a brand'. We are deliberately aiming at a long-term effect. Then, we may use a six-week half life, or ten weeks, or occasionally more.

In between, we can be at a four- to-six-week half-life. This may also represent a mix of short-term and long-term effects.

5 Reaching the same shoppers more than once

Introduction

The question tackled in this chapter has caused even more confusion than disentangling advertising effects over time. Every analyst now believes that there are diminishing returns to increasing amounts of advertising. That is, if you double the amount of advertising a shopper sees, you have less than double the effect.

The disputes are partly about the definitions and techniques to describe a response function. That is, the relationship between increasing advertising weight and the results. Worse, some measures which *look like* response functions turn out not to be. In Part 2, I describe some of the alternative approaches and difficulties; in this chapter I write about my own approach.

The numbers to which I apply this idea are aggregate data; that is, all shoppers are lumped together and it is their total behaviour that is in question. They are not separated, as in Chapter 6, or in Part 2, into separate groups such as light and heavy viewers.

Nor am I describing the result of actual OTS on individuals, which is also covered in the next chapter. I am concerned with the reaction of the average shopper to the current pressure from advertising which adstock represents. Ultimately, my unit is a rating point. As described in the last chapter, to make adstock, recent television ratings have been summed with varying weights – the most recent with a large weight, those many weeks ago with smaller weights. The question is, how does the average shopper react to different adstocks?

There are two distinctions here. First, an opportunity to see takes place in an actual minute and is about the potential viewing of an actual individual. The reaction to adstock is also at a particular time, but is to the cumulated effect of past OTS. And I measure it on the total universe, not on an individual.

My defence of this practice is, first, that it deals with commonly available data: ratings and total sales. I am describing the data which management is familiar with and uncovering the connections. Second, it is not as liable to some of the dangers that dealing with individual data may be subject to. These are described in Part 2. Third, and critically, I am using the units which apply directly to scheduling: the ratings we buy create adstocks, the aggregate sales numbers describe our target for maximisation.

The snag is that my units are abstract. A brand's sales share in a week is not as 'real' as an actual purchase. Adstock is not a concrete ad exposure (incidentally, nor is an opportunity to see). It is tempting to translate adstock in the following way. When we buy 100 ratings, on average a person in our target has a single *opportunity* to see (once more, remember there is a lot of variation round this average).

So when adstock is at 100, this is equivalent on average to an ad exposure rate of one OTS a week. We can understand 'one OTS a week', and I use this way of labelling the first two figures for this chapter. But we have to remember that studying response to different levels of adstock is not identical to looking at numbers of OTS for an individual and the corresponding chances of buying the brand.

Why are diminishing returns needed?

The question, 'How does the average shopper react to different adstocks?' was apparently answered in the last chapter: the larger the adstock, the higher the awareness or the sales of the brand. The relationship there was linear: double the pressure from advertising and these measures also doubled.

As an approximation, this works well most of the time, as the last chapter showed. But it can be no more than an approximation, and linear increase cannot be continued indefinitely.

There are two ways that common sense rejects the idea of linear response continuing indefinitely.

First, imagine a series of experiments for a single week, starting with 100 ratings. Next, 200. Then 400, and so on. Long before we get to 800 or 1,600 ratings, the total reaction of the shopper cannot be a simple multiple of the reaction to the previous experiment. You might get close to double the result, going from 100 to 200. You do not expect 16 times the effect at 1,600 ratings.

Second, imagine a simple schedule of two spots. Consider the choice between two widely separated weeks in which we might buy time, and suppose that the decay is so rapid that the OTS in the first week produces a negligible adstock in the second. The first of these weeks has a slightly higher Value/Cost than the second, so it is our first choice for buying ratings. Where does our second choice fall? If response is linear, the first week will be chosen again, as it still offers better Value/Cost and gives us the better return. So will the third, the fourth choice and so on. The second week will never be chosen, as it always gives a poorer return.

Any planner would reject the over-concentration that this system produces. There must come a point when it is better to buy in the second week, rather than continuing to choose the first. It is this need to allow for diminishing returns (here, in the first week), which makes schedule constructors assume a convex response. The result is to produce schedules which are more spread out.

Why does a linear assumption work quite well when we fit real data, then? Because a gentle curve and a straight line start off (that is, at small values) looking much the same. It is the angle of the response that makes the big difference between fits and schedules, not its shape. It is only when we get to high adstocks, or when diminishing returns are very sharp, that the difference in shape matters very much.

What is the shape of response?

The shape[1] of the curve used here is again called 'geometric'. A couple of examples are shown in Figure 5.1, and they are compared with a straight line.

All three curves in this figure have been standardised to go through a response of two units at a pressure equivalent to two OTS a week, or an adstock equivalent to 200 ratings a week. The one labelled F = 20 (explained below) follows the line rather closely, the other (F = 50) is certainly different, but not so far off that it is likely to give a very different set of results in practice.

A similar shape seems to be given by Zeno's paradox. This concerns the flight of an arrow towards its target. It takes a certain time to go halfway, additional time to go half of the distance remaining, still more for the next

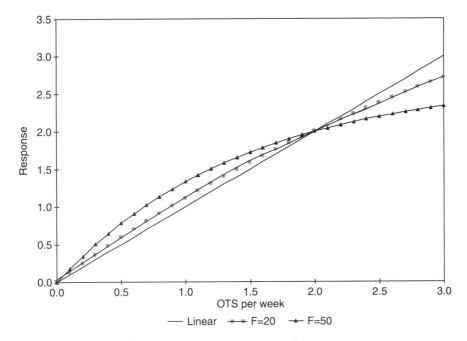

Figure 5.1 Diminishing returns can be close to linear

half...and so on. Hence, apparently but of course wrongly, it can never reach its target.

Suppose response gets halfway to its maximum when a person has one opportunity to see. At the next OTS, it gets half of the distance remaining, at the next OTS, a further half and so on. In this case, response[2] never really gets to the target, but after a few OTS it gets very close.

The two curves of Figure 5.1 are redrawn on a different scale in Figure 5.2, in a way appropriate to Zeno's paradox. This time, the upper limit is taken as the unit. A third is added, labelled F = 80. Clearly there is a range of shapes here, from a near-linear shape (F = 20) to steep diminishing returns (F = 80). Even at F = 80, the shape is close to linear for the small adstocks at the first part of the curve. In practice, on most purchase occasions, adstock is indeed this low. This is why the linear adstock model generally fits well, and is also why the exact shape of diminishing returns is hard to find by modelling.

The unit of advertising pressure for these plots, on the X axis, is given as OTS per week, as pointed out above, the equivalent to TV ratings in a week divided by 100. If the rate of OTS per week is one per week, the height of the curve in Figure 5.2 is written F, as a percentage of the upper limit. If the X axis had been actual OTS, and not OTS per week, this would be the first OTS (hence the choice of 'F' for the parameter). The equation for the curves is given in the notes.[3]

Evidence for diminishing returns

What evidence is there that this sort of convex response actually happens? There are various sources. Some are given in Part 2, but the reader should be warned that they are not all based on the aggregate model for which we are going to apply the curves. The most direct evidence comes from a type of adstock modelling known, naturally, as 'adstock+response'.

We can combine adstocks (from Chapter 4) and the rate of diminishing returns, explained above. We can then calculate a number proportional to the effect of advertising, from any schedule, for subsequent weeks.

The process is first to work out the adstocks each week, for a given half-life. Then, for each week, use diminishing returns, for a given F, to calculate the effect.

The simplest case is to take advertising in a single week. Suppose we had 500 ratings in week 1. For any half-life, we can calculate the resulting adstock. For example, if the half-life is very short, at one week, we get the following adstocks:

Week 1	2	3	4	5	6
250	167	56	19	6	2

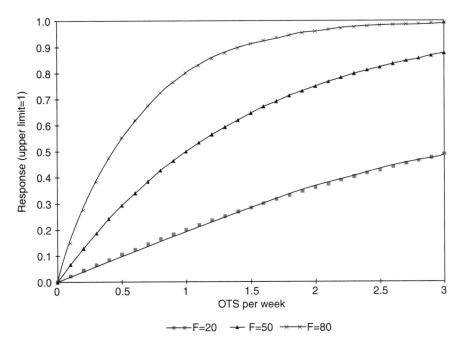

Figure 5.2 Response to increasing advertising pressure

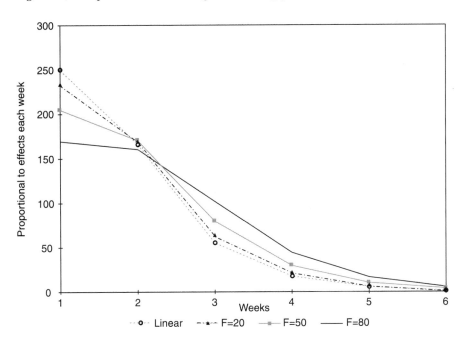

Figure 5.3 Ad effects from 500 GRPs in week 1, Half-life = 1 week for different rates of diminishing returns

If response is linear, we get the 'linear' response in Figure 5.3 each week. It is simply a plot of the adstocks. But for the rates of diminishing returns investigated above, the shape is different (when standardised so that the total is 500, as for linear response). Figure 5.3 shows that as F gets larger, and diminishing returns get steeper, the curve flattens out. But notice that the curves are not as different as you might have expected from Figure 5.2. With linear response, we got half the total effect in the first week. When as much as 80 per cent of the maximum response is at the rate of one OTS a week, we still get 41 per cent of the total effect in the first week.

It is only when the pressure is high (above the rate of one OTS per week) that the different curves begin to have a noticeable effect. Additionally, if I had used a longer half-life than one week (even three or four weeks), the resulting adstocks, even from 500 ratings, would not have been so high as to be much affected by diminishing returns. The decisions about diminishing returns are therefore very dependent on the actual ratings that are common in the country you are working in.

I have said that the exact rate of diminishing returns is quite hard to measure in practice. But the argument used about the need for some diminishing returns in schedule construction – to prevent all the money being spent in the best week – shows that we must prefer some assumption of this kind to linear response.

Estimating the rate of diminishing returns

Now that the parameter F has been explained, I turn to the question of estimating it. This section and the examples are for technical readers only.

It would be possible to estimate the half-life and F simultaneously. This can be done with a table showing the goodness of fit when both are varied, and the highest point on this surface is then identified. Or, there are other more sophisticated techniques for finding the optimum fit directly.

In practice, I rarely use either of these. The first, because it is laborious, and a simpler method works as well; the second, because I lose the information about the sensitivity of the result, and I can no longer make a joint estimation when I need the half-life or F to be the same for several brands.

I explained in Chapter 4 that, for scheduling, quite a rough estimate of half-life is adequate. The same is true for diminishing returns, which are even harder to estimate. We cannot use a linear shape in scheduling, but all that is really important is to distinguish near-linear, moderate and steeply diminishing returns.

Example: over-the-counter pharmaceutical products

Two brands are studied in this example, with 65 weeks of data. There was not much variation in sales share, but satisfactory t-values[4] were obtained for estimates of the effects. As well as the brand's own advertising, individual competitors' advertising had detectable effects; so did product formulation changes.

For Brand A we would pick a two-week or three-week half-life; for Brand B, between three and six. Having chosen the best half-life, the following R-squareds[4] were found for different values of F:

F	40	50	60	70	80	90
Brand A	0.621	0.622	0.622	0.622	0.621	0.616
Brand B	0.698	0.704	0.711	0.719	0.728	0.738

The rate of diminishing returns is harder to choose than say, the half-life in the awareness example in Chapter 4, since the values of R-squared are not very different. The reason is the similarity of the response curves in plots like Figure 5.1. We are going to get only indications of the shape, not a precise estimate – but that, as pointed out above, is all that scheduling requires.

In this case, we can only say Brand A has diminishing returns of middling steepness (F = 50 to 70), but for Brand B response is steep and a large F must be chosen.

In this case, the fits were also calculated for the full set of combinations of half-life and of F. Instead of picking the best half-life for the linear fit and then finding the best F, it was possible to find the best combination. For both brands the results were identical and we need not have bothered to calculate the full table.

Using single-source data

Exactly the same adstock modelling should be applied to data derived from a panel of shoppers who also record their viewing. It is inefficient merely to count OTS in an interval before a purchase and think that this represents current advertising pressure. There are no new technical problems, though individual panel data require considerably more processing.

In an IRI BehaviorScan ketchup example,[5] the half-life was first chosen for the effects of Heinz and of Hunts advertising on their respective sales. It was two weeks – not a rapid decay for the daily data I had in this case. Other factors taken into account in the estimating procedure were a trend term, price relative to the category average and competitors' advertising. From the table in Chapter 4, we see that the equivalent for the weekly intervals used in scheduling would be about two-and-a-half weeks.

In order to investigate diminishing returns, the regressions were repeated with various values of F as well as with linear response. This time the t-values are used to identify the best choice. This is equivalent to using R-squareds, and although R-squareds were used above and are conventional, t-values are recommended.

F	linear	10	20	30	40	50	60
Heinz	3.0	2.6	2.2	1.8	1.4	1.1	0.9
Hunts	2.7	3.0	3.1	3.2	3.2	3.2	3.1

There is again a difference here between brands. For Heinz, a linear fit is best (3.0 is the highest t-value); for scheduling we would use a near linear shape. For Hunts, we are directed to a gentle convex shape (since 3.2 is the t-value for F = 30, 40 and 50); for scheduling we would assume 40% of maximum response at the rate of one OTS a week.

Zielske (continued)

In the last chapter I concluded that Zielske's experiment suggested a half-life of five weeks for his campaign. I now apply the idea of diminishing returns to the adstock.

There are two numbers needed to calculate the relative effect of different amounts of adstock. First, what is the maximum our score can reach – in this case the percentage recalling the ads? Second, what percentage of this maximum is reached when adstock is at the rate of one OTS in a week?

I can calculate the adstocks at each of the weeks when there were interviews, and then choose[6] the maximum and the diminishing returns parameter F so that the observed and fitted recalls are as close as possible.

Clearly the maximum percentage recall is 100 or less. Because there is an absolute limit, I expect the diminishing returns curve to be steep, which is in fact the case. It is unrealistic to deduce that the same must be true for effects on most brands' sales shares, which are far from any conceivable limit.

I concluded that maximum recall was 95% and that diminishing returns were indeed steep with F = 80. The predictions for recall for both schedules are given in Figure 5.4.

Is Value/Cost adequate?

Now that we have a model which spreads the effect of advertising over subsequent weeks, I return to the Value/Cost calculation which evaluated the

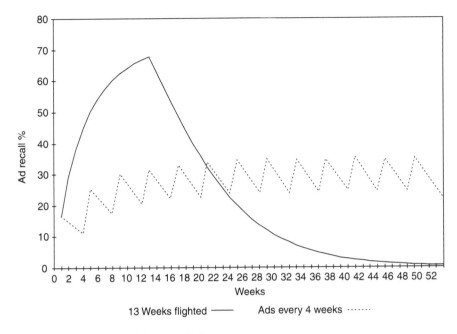

Figure 5.4 Fit to Zielske recall data

different weeks of the year at the end of Chapter 3. It is now clear why I then said this was an approximate evaluation.

We do not get all the effect of spending money in a particular week during the week itself. Some of the effect occurs in subsequent weeks, and these may not all have the same values. Now that we know how to allow for this, and for diminishing returns as well, I return to the valuation of individual weeks. The way to do this is also a good introduction to Chapter 7.

Suppose there is a standard number of ratings which we might place in any of the 52 weeks. For any half-life and F-value, we can calculate the subsequent effect, in the same way as we did above for the 500 ratings in week 1.

But these effects are worth more or less to us, depending on the values we have placed on these weeks. The overall benefit we get (disregarding for a moment how much money we have had to lay out) must be the sum, over subsequent weeks, of the size of the advertising effect times the value of the relevant week.

Suppose, for example, the standard number of ratings was 500, and the half-life was one week, then the table opposite gave us the adstocks in following weeks. Suppose diminishing returns were such that F=50, then the next line in the table overleaf is proportional to the effect in these weeks.

Now add our information about the values of these weeks. Let weeks 1 and 2 have double the value of later weeks. This information is also shown in the table.

Now multiply the effects and the values of these weeks and sum the result. In a real calculation the numbers would not be rounded as they are here, and the sum continues to the end of the year (and there is an adjustment for year-end effects). With these figures, the sum or benefit is 871 (this is 204x2 +170x2 +79x1 + ...).

Compare this with the result of spending the 500 ratings in week 2. All the figures are the same, starting in week 2, except that the value in the week after the TV burst is only one. The sum falls to 701. The adstock resulting is the same, but the half which fell into the subsequent week met lower values.

Clearly we are better off spending our money in week 1 rather than week 2, if the costs in these weeks are the same. Value/Cost could not have told us this: it would have evaluated the two weeks as equal.

Week	1	2	3	4	5	6
Adstock	250	167	56	19	6	2
Effect	204	170	79	30	10	4
Value	2	2	1	1	1	1

The new evaluation of weeks

We can now be more exact in our evaluation than we were in Chapter 3. What practical differences do we expect?

Again, we buy some standard number of ratings in a particular week; this time, say a more realistic 100. We know how much it would cost to do this. The result would be to create and spread adstocks over this and later weeks. It is these adstocks which create the sales effects, mediated as we have just seen by diminishing returns. In each of the weeks where we now expect a sales effect, the value of that week will make it a small or a large one.

The process of evaluating the benefit, or return on our investment, from that week is as follows. Note the cost. For the following weeks, calculate adstocks. Apply diminishing returns. Multiply the result by the values of the weeks. Sum over the following weeks in the year. Divide by the cost in order to see how much return we got per dollar or per pound.

What do I mean by 'return', knowing that some adstock will be left over? Total adstocks equal the 100 ratings we start with. The benefit we got during the year come from only the proportion (100 – left over)/100 of the spend. So we should not actually divide by the whole cost – only by this proportion of it.

This calculation sounds lengthy, but like everything else in this problem, can be programmed and is then a speedy operation. Is it worth doing? That is, are the results different from the simple Value/Cost sum?

The answer is that, for short half-lives, like a week or a little longer, it is usually not worth doing. But with a medium or long-term half-life, say four weeks or more, the calculation can make a difference to the evaluation of a single week. The difference is usually below 10 per cent so it is not too serious.

For a dramatic distribution of values, the results can make the difference between using a week and not using it. In an example in Chapter 7, where advertising is to support the promotion, the week before the promotion starts was given zero value. Hence its Value/Cost is also zero and you might think it would never be used. Some planners would indeed never place advertising there. But with sufficiently low costs the week before the promotion, and because the bulk of the adstock created at that time ran over the duration of the promotion, it could be sensible to advertise then.

Example of the new evaluation

The evaluation given at the end of Chapter 3 is repeated. But this time, assume a half-life of six weeks, and a rate of diminishing returns such that half the maximum is reached at a rate of one OTS a week.

The result is in the last column of Table 3.1 (pp. 34–5), and the two evaluations are compared in Figure 5.5.

With a half-life this long, the process is always looking well forward, to see what will be achieved later, by advertising this week. The first nine weeks give a clear demonstration. Neither values nor costs vary much, so the Value/Cost line is rather steady. But values are just about to increase (from 77 to 108 in the first week of March). The nearer we get to this week, the higher the return we expect from March.

During March, costs are rising, because viewing decreases. May is similar, and also provides poorer Value/Cost generally, because costs are higher. The Value/Cost line shows these as abrupt changes. However, the adstock model smoothes out the jump up in March and the fall in April. The trend is slightly up in April, anticipating the good values to come between May and July.

September shows the reverse. Value/Cost rises slightly, as viewing increases. But the adstock model anticipates poor values ahead in October and November.

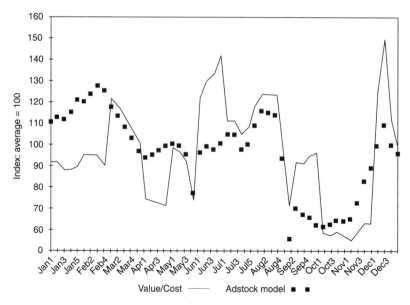

Figure 5.5 Two ways to compare the efficiency of weeks

Conclusions on diminishing returns

We have a method which estimates the rate of diminishing returns; it can do this with normal time series or with single-source data. It is adequate for identifying whether we have an extreme or a mid-position – and both types have been found.

The weight and effectiveness of the advertising, and the brand situation, together determine what sort of response the advertising gets. That is, whether diminishing returns are steeply convex (and little or no repetition is needed), or whether returns are near linear.

Estimating half-life and the rate of diminishing returns
At the end of Chapter 4, I suggested we need a method to decide which examples of decay are nearest our own case, when we have to guess what half-life applies to a particular brand and campaign. Exactly the same is true for its rate of diminishing returns.

The method recommended is a battery of scales, in language the planner understands, and which are scored for the brand and campaign. For example, 'The share objective is ... maintaining share ... or increasing share', 'and 'The main communication is ... new news ... or already established'. The scores have been calibrated from a set of modelled examples. In a new application the answers are weighted and summed, to give an index used to set an appropriate half-life and rate of diminishing returns.[7]

6 Buying and the cover criterion

New data, new criteria

We now enter a different world. In previous chapters, the object was to improve the cost-effectiveness of the media plan in its purpose – improving sales. The schedule was a tool for selling as much of the brand as possible with a fixed advertising budget. Here, it is pure media measures which concern us, numbers whose purpose is to be currency for media negotiations, not to indicate sales effects. We are talking cost per thousand, cover of the target audience and so on. Because the criteria are less clear, and the objectives are indirect (not sales themselves), the arguments in this chapter are sometimes fuzzy. There is more on these difficulties in Part 2.

The data source in this chapter is an industry panel. Households or individuals report their TV viewing, which is taken as representative of a country or region. There are no brand-purchase data. The panel can be segmented in various ways, and reports are then about particular demographic groups, usually crude approximations to our real target. For instance, the examples in Chapter 2 were about homemakers or housewives.

Of course the people handling these data are well aware that sales or some behavioural change are the real purpose. But in pure media evaluations, progress towards this objective cannot be measured. The traditional media numbers, like the cover achieved, take over as ends in themselves.

The criteria used to judge buying include administrative skills. Buyers have to draw up their plans quickly and accurately, they have to forecast, they have to spend the budgets at the agreed time, they have to negotiate successfully when plans are changed, when late money is found or when budgets are reduced. These skills are necessary.

But it is on costs and cover that buyers are mainly judged. It is thought easier to evaluate buying, rather than TV planning, because data are available which seem to do this job.

There is a dilemma in much media planning. Should I do what I believe is best for the brand? Or should I meet the pure media criteria? These are not always the same. The planner and buyer ask themselves whether they are really working for the marketing director or for the media controller.

Given a fixed budget, the cost criterion means buying more ratings (of the agreed type) than a competitor – but not so many more than estimated as to show the forecasting was faulty.

Maximising the ratings achieved, or buying at the lowest possible rates, sounds like a straightforward objective. It is complicated in two ways. First, by a 'quality' definition. This can have several meanings. It is an attempt to get sales-effectiveness back into the system through some evaluation of:

– dayparts (do homemakers pay less attention to the set in daytime, so commercials placed there are less effective?)
– the position of the ad in the break (do we reach viewers before they may switch over?)
– the programmes the ad is in (do more of 'our sort' of homemakers watch them?)

Regulations on TV advertising may have a similar effect – not transmitting ads about sanitary protection, for example, at times when a family audience is thought to find them embarrassing.

Deciding what 'quality' means, and applying such rules, are important decisions. They are treated here simply as one of the special conditions governing buying for a particular advertiser.

Do not forget that apparently hard numbers, like, '60 per cent reached', conceal uncertainties in the research operation. As Gus Priemer[1] pointed out, much of this 60 per cent is in fact untouched by our advertising. Nevertheless, such numbers from industry research are all we have.

The cover criterion

There is one particular characteristic of TV viewing which makes it unrealistic to set cost as the only criterion: different people watch different amounts of television. We divide people into three groups by the amount they view, and then look at the averages for the three groups. We find that the light viewers watch less than an hour a day and the middle group watch for about two hours. Some of the heavy viewers have the set on for as many as six hours a day; this may be for other people to watch, or just for company and occasional attention.

Two-thirds of all viewing is by heavy viewers. People in this group are often those who do not go out of the house much and in fact do less of nearly everything – except watch TV. The couch potato is not an attractive target for many advertisers, so times of day when heavy viewers form a majority of the audience are those least in demand and the cheapest to buy.

When a buyer is judged solely on cost, and there are no 'quality' or other restrictions, the Law of Unintended Consequences applies. He buys first those times of day just described. Many of these opportunities to see are on the same people, who are hit time and again. We saw in the last chapter that this often means overkill. Meanwhile, some desirable viewers, more active and harder to reach, see few if any of our ads. These results were not expected from the brief.

The advertiser therefore realises that getting a large number of OTS in total is not enough as the only criterion. He wants a lot of people seeing his ads, and he wants them paying attention to the set when his ad is on. In addition to low cost, and in addition to 'quality', he needs some other criterion to judge the buyer.

The definitions are simple. First, we need a 'reporting period', the time over which cover is calculated. Take a month as a typical period (some argue that weeks should be used). Second, consider the individuals in the viewing panel who are agreed to approximate our target, and again I take home-makers. Each of them is treated as of equal value, since we know nothing about their shopping habits. Finally, go through the spots bought in our campaign and check whether, according to the viewing data, each individual saw none, just one, just two, and so on.

This is a frequency distribution. Here are the percentages of the target you might get at various OTS frequencies from 200 GRPs:

OTS	0	1	2	3	4+
Percentage of target	39	25	14	8	14

When you count the homemakers by whether they saw at least so many spots, you get the corresponding cumulative or cover distribution:

OTS	1+	2+	3+	4+
Percentage of target	61	3	22	14

Two important descriptions of repetition have now been stated. First, repetition of *what*? In this chapter, opportunities to see. Second, repetition *over how long*? Here, over a period of one month. In Part 2 we learn that users of the idea of diminishing returns have not always been too scrupulous about defining this interval. For us, it is always part of the initial conditions which are specified when a schedule is being planned. Clearly it makes a difference whether the reporting period is one month, or a week.

Note that the people who fall into these cells are individuals who are very likely to differ by their weight of viewing TV. Those who saw no commercials are probably light viewers; those who saw four or more, heavy viewers.

It hardly needs saying that the 39 per cent in the table above cannot be affected by advertising at all, so no advertiser wants to see a high figure in this box.

It *looks* as though the non-covered are like the people at the left-hand end of Figures 5.1 and 5.2 (pp. 57 and 59), at zero OTS per week.

But the definitions in those plots were very different. They were about giving the *same* group of people a lower or a higher advertising pressure. At a heading like 'two OTS a week', we meant that this was the average amount. Of course heavy viewers saw more and light viewers less, but in comparison with the heading 'one OTS a week' *everyone* got twice as much pressure.

Thus in Chapter 5 I was discussing 'response functions' – how the whole population responded to more or to less advertising pressure. In the tables above, those at two OTS certainly saw twice as many of our ads as those at one OTS, but they were not the same people having double the pressure. They are also likely to differ in their shopping habits, as we see in Chapter 11.

This misunderstanding has muddied the water when some researchers have tried to measure 'response functions'. They think they are describing the effect of more OTS, when they are actually describing heavy viewers.

Of course, it is possible to have response functions for individuals. But these have to be measured by an experiment – not just by observing, among a mixed group of people, those who had no OTS, those who had one and so on.

It is likely that light viewers react to a lower level of exposures, a common idea for which support is quoted later. If a shopper sees few ads in total, a single exposure is likely to seize a higher 'share of mind' as they are also seeing less of competitors' advertising.

But the table above is often talked about as though it *did* describe a response function. It is also implied that by changing the details of the buying, the channels, the dayparts and so on, we can give the *same* people more ad exposure or less. This is unlikely to be so and we must be on our guard against this mistake so I repeat my point:

> When we use the industry viewing panel, and as we go from left to right on the OTS table, we are *not* seeing *only* the effect of more advertising exposure.

Buyers concentrate mainly on two objectives: shoppers getting enough OTS in the reporting interval – but not getting too much, because buyers believe diminishing returns will reduce the effect.

They are correct in being worried about the left-hand cell – those who saw no commercials. Clearly we have not affected them at all. They are also correct about the extreme right-hand end, but for a different reason. If an excessive proportion of the ratings bought comes from very heavy viewers, this throws doubt on the kind of time the buyer has got.

To sum up, buyers are not correct if they use the frequency distribution in these two ways: as a substitute for 'quality' measures which are better specified directly, or as data to which they apply diminishing returns measures drawn from a different source (for example, an analysis of purchase occasions when informants were weighted by frequency of purchase).

The right way to use the cover criterion

The advertiser wants a lot of ratings, of course, but he does not want them all at the right-hand end of the OTS distribution. Hence, it is normal to set an objective at the light-exposure end, some minimum percentage which the buyer should achieve. If the above table reports an average performance, the advertiser might set a target above the norm, for example, 'At least 65 per cent at one-plus', or, 'At least 40 per cent at two-plus'.

From the way TV viewing works, it is usually the case that buys which push up the percentage at one-plus or two-plus mean that you have less money to spend on other spots which add mainly at the high-frequency end. Hence, paying attention to the left-hand end prevents the buyer from concentrating on the easier and cheaper OTS at higher frequencies.

Sometimes, a range is set instead of a minimum. For example, 'At least 50 per cent in two to four OTS'. The 'four' in this criterion implies that five or more OTS are worth nothing. This is not recommended, and the following example is one way of showing why. Suppose I am offered a free spot which would increase my two-plus by 2 per cent and my five-plus by 3 per cent. The result is to drop my two to four OTS by 1 per cent. Should I refuse the spot? Of course not. Stressing the low-frequency requirement and insisting on the percentage at 2+ automatically reduces the high frequencies; there is no need to value them at zero.

Even if we cannot separate an effect of frequency from an effect of weight of viewing, it is, as I have pointed out, undeniable that those on the left have had a lower frequency of exposure. If we believe in diminishing returns for individuals, we do not want to reach people very often in the reporting period. We would rather reach someone else for the first time, so it is reasonable to try to increase the number on the left of the table, if necessary at some expense to those on the right.

We are unable to directly apply the conclusions of Chapter 5 (about steep or near-linear response in a particular case), owing to the interference of weight of viewing in these tables. But the view we reach, about the shape of response, could have an effect on what cover criterion we choose. The steeper the rate of diminishing returns, the more likely we are to suggest a low OTS number. In practice, over a month, the criterion is often two, three or four. Over a week it is usually one. This choice is a management decision, based on the ideas above. It is not a direct conclusion from research into sales effects.

Once having set the criterion, there is still the target percentage to set – the percentage over the cover criterion. The target percentage will vary with the budget available – the more ratings we can buy, the higher the target should be. Again, there is no general answer. Normal management practice varies between setting an average number based on previous local experience (expecting it to be exceeded about half the time), and raising the bar (to encourage even harder efforts from the buyer).

This is a difficult subject to discuss, because it looks as though I am considering again the possibility that advertising suffers from diminishing returns. This is, in fact, the way most people think about the OTS distribution. But I believe that this source cannot be used for a diminishing-returns analysis.

There are two different situations. In Chapter 5, I was thinking about the effect of *increasing adstock* on the aggregate, or, if you prefer, on the average shopper. Now, the possibility is that the *repetition* of OTS on *individuals* (as seen in the viewing panel) has the same sort of danger.

What criterion?

Tradition plays more of a part than argument in choosing the actual criterion. The information available on the importance of light viewers, or the effects of high attention and relevant programming, is rarely sufficient to provide either an obvious criterion or a percentage figure to aim at. Nevertheless, the reasons for emphasising the importance of light viewers or for having some cover criterion are sensible; the number chosen (in our present state of ignorance) is less important than exercising some management control.

What does the buyer do when he has been set an objective like 'At least 40 per cent at two-plus'? There are some obvious tricks, like placing two spots on one evening, which increases the chance of a viewer seeing both. Or, buying into series which, he believes (not always correctly), have high overlap between episodes.

Today, he can turn to computer programs[2] which review the history of the viewing panel. These 'optimisers' can find the combinations of channel, daypart and programmes which meet the reach or cover criterion most economically. If not all of these spots are actually buyable, he at least gets an idea about the channels and times to aim at. If the inventory is a realistic one, he gets an ideal spot list.

Another device – as a realistic schedule is added to – is to analyse the viewing data by the cover added, at the frequency chosen. The table opposite gives a simple example for 3+ cover, as the GRPs increase from 0 to 400. The cover added at each step of 50 GRPs has been calculated; so has the cost of each added cover point.

Because of the shape of this cover curve, plotted against the GRPs which caused it, the amount of cover added at each step *increases* to 250 GRPs. From 300 to 400 GRPs, the amount of cover added gradually *decreases*. The last column repeats the message: the cost of adding cover falls up to 250 GRPs, and then increases. If we want to buy 3+ cover, a burst of 200 or 250 GRPs looks sensible, since the added cover is cheapest there.

GRPs	*3+ cover*	*Added cover*	*Cost per added cover point*
0	0.0	0.0	0
50	4.7	4.7	212
100	10.3	5.6	178
150	16.6	6.2	160
200	23.1	6.6	153
250	29.7	6.6	152
300	36.0	6.3	159
350	41.6	5.7	176
400	46.4	4.8	209

This argument has to be treated with care. For example, two bursts of 200 GRPs actually buy a lower percentage of those who reached 3+ (twice 23.1 is 46.2, and many of these will be the same people) than a burst of 400 (46.4). The reason is that starting a new burst returns us initially to a situation of a high cost per added cover point.

However, it remains true that tables like this can support setting a maximum for GRPs in a reporting period. For instance, we might conclude that we do not want more than 300 GRPs in the reporting period.

Incidentally, the relationship between the first two columns of this table is called a 'cover guide'. For the restrictions set by a given advertiser, and for a particular skill or practice in buying, there is high stability in the relationships between the GRPs bought and the percentage meeting the various cover criteria. Traditionally, there are differences by country, by time of year, by the channels used, by target audience and so on. These differences can be less than sometimes supposed. In any case, differences from an average can be found by analysing actual schedules; then, an appropriate allowance can be made for a schedule still to be bought but using the same buying restrictions as the schedules analysed.

Such a table can be used to tell us the minimum number of GRPs for a particular cover criterion to be met with confidence. For example, to have at least 30 per cent at 3+, the table says we need about 250 ratings.

Effective frequency – the wrong mental model

This section covers points discussed again in Part 2. I try to treat the situation here in general terms, while later in the book I describe actual research and deductions. Some of the points have been expanded elsewhere,[3] and commented on in the industry.[4]

Once the cover criterion is set, it is often called the 'effective frequency'. One reason for this phrase is obvious. If the advertiser evaluates you on the percentage above this frequency, he seems to be thinking of it as the 'effective' one. The word cannot have its normal meaning as in 'sales-effective', as though any lower frequency had no effect. Clearly all frequencies of exposure have some effect. This leads naturally to the next point.

The other reason advanced for setting a cover criterion is diminishing returns. Of course diminishing returns exist. They can be measured. They are a necessary part of scheduling, as discussed in Chapter 5. But it has to be said again that the definition used there for a response function – the reaction of the same person, or of the overall average, to increasing pressure from advertising – *cannot* be used on the viewing-panel data. It is not just that we have no data from this panel about shopping. The point is that when we compare two cells we are not dealing with the same people, or the average person, being shifted up to a higher level of OTS. They are *different* people – those in the cell to the right are heavier viewers. It is not legitimate to use the viewing-panel data as if they could be the basis of a response function.

Consider the following table, where the second row contains the sales share of my brand for the individuals who fell into the cells on the first row, which shows the number of OTS they saw. To make the figures easier to read, the sales shares have been indexed on the share for those who had no OTS.

OTS	0	1	2	3	4+
Sales share index	100	110	118	123	128

Suppose these data came from an experiment, in which the first group saw no OTS, the second group was identical in every way except that that they were exposed to a single OTS, and so on. This *would* then be a response function, with a typical convex shape.

But suppose instead we had some way[5] of measuring our sales to members of the industry viewing panel. And suppose the table came from that source. What can we conclude? This is no longer an experiment. It is 'data as they fall'. We know that there are more heavy viewers on the right. It is feasible (in fact, likely) that we are seeing an association between weight of viewing and the likelihood of buying the brand. This could be all we are seeing – and not an advertising effect. We just do not know how much of this buying is association with weight of viewing, and how much is caused by advertising.

Unfortunately, the table *looks* identical for these two incompatible situations. In the first, a real effect has been measured. In the second, the table just describes the way people fall into the cells, and what their purchasing average is.

Many people do indeed think about the OTS frequency analysis for their campaign as though it were a report on an experiment. Normally, they know there is increasing response to increasing OTS (on the same person, or on average). Whatever they think this sort of increase is, they believe it can be applied to the cells in the table.

If the increase is steep (and Chapter 5 showed this can happen), then the value to the advertiser of people on the right of the table is little more than those in the middle (because the curve is flat for people on the right). Hence, it is argued, the spots which got the high repetition on the right of the table are wasteful. The money would be better spent increasing the number of people in the middle or at the left-hand end. The argument is weak in two ways. First, you cannot actually move OTS from one position on the table to another: OTS on the right are cheaper than on the left. Second, people on the right of the table are heavy viewers who react differently to repetition from those on the left.

Conclusions

1. For good reasons, it is normal practice to set the buyer a cover criterion. The example here is, 'Over a month when you are on air, get at least 40 per cent of the homemaker viewers to see two or more spots.'

2. For the particular circumstances of the campaign, it is recommended you choose a cover criterion based on the total ratings bought, a view on the importance of cover or of frequency, and previous experience of operating

this criterion. Similarly, the target to set for the percentage of the distribution above the criterion should be based on experience and management style.

3. In achieving a particular cover criterion, buying skills play a large part, but a bigger factor is the budget, and the number of GRPs we expect to buy in the reporting period.

4. It is reasonable to set the criterion at a low number (one or two, perhaps even four for a large burst). The efforts to meet this criterion will normally do more good than lowering overall costs by increasing the tail of the distribution of OTS. Forcing the buyer to look for cover is expected to cut some of the high numbers.

5. There are few firm grounds, if any, for choosing the cover criterion. We are not talking the language of sales-effectiveness now. This is a management decision, based partly and insecurely on a view about the shape of diminishing returns, but mainly on the relative importance of light viewers and being covered at all, and on the quality of TV time.

6. There is no accepted way to compare the two sorts of criterion – the estimated sales effect of the schedule, discussed in the previous chapters, and the control of the buyer discussed here. A compromise is suggested later, but the problem is one the industry has not yet solved.

7. Many people will find this chapter difficult. This is because they believe, without having looked at it too closely, that a response function they can use for their brand has already been estimated (by someone else). Furthermore, they think it can be applied to the viewing-panel data. Therefore they believe they can safely set an effective frequency. My own view is that this argument is wrong.

7   The solution

Introduction

Some readers will understand why Gus Priemer wrote, 'sound theory, defensible logic and probable effectiveness – these values have no place in advertising.'

It is my hope that such cynicism is not applied to this chapter, where I describe my own recommendation, the way I think the scheduling problem should be resolved. It draws together the last five chapters.

I have spelled out the 'sound theory' which is my theory on how I think advertising often works and how its effects can be modelled. I now use what I believe is defensible logic to deduce how to write a schedule that aims at probable effectiveness.

I am well aware that, as well as cynicism, I have to face the charge of complexity. I plead guilty – it is the sensible reaction to a complex situation in real life. But it is complex only when you peer under the bonnet, as we shall do together here. To the user of the programs BAT (Budget Allocation over Time) or SWriter™, the process is no more complex than any other part of media planning.

The special input the planner provides is in two parts, corresponding to the VC-DD model.

Values and *costs* are the environment in which the schedule has to be written. The first job is to specify these and, as we have seen, this is not too hard.

The rates of *decay* and of *diminishing returns* are then key to the individual solution. I know they are rarely determined exactly. They are, however, statements about the shape of the schedule you think appropriate to the brand and the creative objective. You can write better schedules, after deciding what sort of reaction you expect to your campaign (you can also calculate the implications of this decision in a more straightforward way).

The process now described gets the justification for laying the schedule out in the form of a table. It is in a form you can discuss rationally. You can assess alternatives. Also, the arithmetic involved is easy to handle when it is in the right place – the computer.

You now know I will ask you to start scheduling with input based on what you have read so far – chosen to represent your own situation. There is then a single *process* for writing the schedule. There are different *outputs*, each appropriate to its own situation.

The process can be applied in three ways.

- Evaluation: you can now answer the questions, 'Is this schedule more efficient than that? Is there a big difference or is it trivial?'
- Improvement: 'How can I make this schedule better?' These are the functions of the program BAT (Budget Allocation over Time).
- My schedule-writing program, SWriter™, which carries out *construction*, and answers the challenge, 'Show me a recommended schedule.'

Specifying the problem

Suppose we have assembled the material needed to evaluate – and to construct – a schedule. A summary follows. I give the name used in this chapter for each item, and a brief reminder or description.

Costs

For each week, we know what we have to pay to buy TV ratings on our target audience (Chapter 2).

Values

For each week, we have determined the value to the advertiser of putting advertising pressure on shoppers (Chapter 3).

Previous and obligatory ratings

We need to take into account the previous rate of advertising. Strictly, this means adstock at the week before our first week; roughly, it means the average rate of GRPs per week for some time before the year we are planning – 'some time' being a week or two for short half-lives, two or three months for long half-lives. This number starts off the adstocks calculation.

For some weeks we may have decided, or had imposed on us, GRPs we simply have to buy (Chapter 3).

Half-lives

The rate of decay of effects from the OTS in any week has been chosen – that is, how the effect is spread over later weeks. The description used is the half-life for adstock. There may be a single assumption here, or we may want to use both a short-term and a long-term effect, in which case the importance we place on each sort has been decided (Chapter 4).

Diminishing returns

In a single week, the way the average shopper reacts to increasing pressure from advertising has been chosen – this may be close to a linear response, or there may be sharply diminishing returns, or something in between. The description used is the parameter F, the percentage of maximum response reached when the rate of adstock is one OTS a week (Chapter 5).

Cover criterion

The buyer has been set a reach or cover criterion, in the OTS distribution, over some reporting period, to ensure that when we are on air we get a minimum particular sort of reach and frequency. In practice, at the scheduling stage, this means a minimum number of ratings for weeks we are on air. Later, when buying decisions are being made, more detail is needed (Chapter 6).

Maximum ratings

As well as a minimum, it may be necessary to specify a maximum number of ratings bought in any one week (Chapter 6).

This looks quite a complicated situation, especially as some of the variables (costs, values) are not described by a mathematical function. Our method has to cope with gritty detail.

Writing a schedule which balances all these criteria is done every day by common sense. But we want to do better than finding a feasible, traditional solution.

Two ways to solve the problem

Both the approaches recommended depend on being able to specify how well a schedule will perform. The criterion is set in the same way as, when modelling, we estimated how well advertising has helped with sales or other behavioural objectives. That is done using adstock. An identical process is followed when predicting the effectiveness of a schedule.

So I start with the method[1] of *evaluating* any schedule. Once we have this we can compare scheduling strategies. It turns out we can also use the method to improve on any suggested solution. At the end of Chapter 5 the foundation of the method was described. Here I turn to its application.

The second approach *constructs* a schedule. I use a technique which will provide a very good, and often optimum, solution. It is called 'hill-climbing' or 'stepwise construction', and that is the subject of the second half of this chapter.

EVALUATION:
How to calculate the effectiveness of a schedule

It is essential that we can work out, for any schedule, a number which represents its sales-effectiveness. By now, you will know what is coming, as I went through the same process at the end of Chapter 5.

I start here with the assumption that there is only one decay rate. From the schedule, I calculate the adstock each week, using the appropriate half-life. Using the formula for diminishing returns, I find what the effect is, each week. But the weeks may not be of equal value to the advertiser, so I multiply the effect by the value of the week. Then I add up these value-weighted effects.

This sum is the sales-effectiveness of the schedule.

There are three complications which have to be taken care of. First, what are the units for effectiveness? Second, won't the beginning of the year always be favoured, because there is then the whole year over which the benefits are felt? Third, what if we are using two different half-lives?

Units for effectiveness

I start by working out the effectiveness of a standard schedule. The standard schedule I choose spends the same amount of money as the one evaluated. Its ratings are in proportion to the Values/Costs. That is, at 'good times' to advertise (high values, low costs), there are more ratings. With large budgets, this is often itself a practical and very effective schedule (especially when half-lives are short and diminishing returns are steep).

The effectiveness of any subsequent schedule is divided by the effectiveness of the standard schedule and multiplied by 100. 'Effectiveness' is therefore an index, comparing our schedule with a standard schedule, and one which is appropriate for our special conditions (the same budget, the same values and costs, the same half-life and diminishing returns).

What do these units *mean*? The answer is that they are proportional to the sales effects of advertising. If one schedule has effectiveness 10 per cent higher than another, we expect the sales related to advertising to be 10 per cent higher too. We do not know, without more information, exactly how much this is. To state this, we need to have done adstock modelling which determined the actual sales effects of advertising. But for schedule construction, this is not relevant. There is some constant we happen not to know, but which does not affect which is the best schedule.

Occasionally, there are other objectives. If the data we used in modelling were about an awareness score, for example, the effectiveness is in increasing this score.

Left-overs

Any schedule produces adstock which will run over into the following year; it has effects beyond the year we are planning. TV ratings early in the year produce adstock which is mostly over during the same year – especially when half-life is short. Late in the year, a lot of the adstock is left over after the current year – especially when half-life is long.

Since adstock in total always equals the ratings which produced it, a simple sum shows how much of it is left over. Total adstock during the year, divided by the total ratings which produced it, is the fraction of the adstock produced during the year which has a benefit in the same year. The complement of this is the proportion left over.

Given a certain effectiveness, I divide it by the fraction just explained. This ensures that if a lot of the effect is actually felt after the year, I have compensated for the left-overs.

Short-term and long-term effects

Suppose I want to know what the immediate effects are, for example, with a half-life of only a week. Then I run the evaluation for this half-life. If I also want to know long-term effects, I simply evaluate with a long half-life. For an overall evaluation, I have to combine the two in the proportion stated.

Scheduling and the cover criterion

In the previous chapter, the status of a percentage of the target audience above some cover figure (such as two-plus) was explained. It is a management decision controlling the kind of time the buyer chooses. How does it compare with the effectiveness figure just described?

Effectiveness is appropriate when the results on sales are being discussed. However, we are not so certain about how to measure this that we can neglect the cover criterion. GRPs do differ in the sort of audience they reach, and to rely on a model using only adstock based on average GRPs may be unwise. Therefore, using both criteria is normal.

The two criteria depend on each other. If we allow flighting, with larger numbers of GRPs when on air, a cover criterion will then be easier to meet. But if there are few GRPs in the reporting period, hitting the cover target will be hard.

We learned from the previous chapter that knowing the GRPs in the reporting period, a reasonable estimate of the percentage past the cover criterion can be made. It is important that this is appropriate to the buying methods which will actually be used. We can set a number of GRPs in the period which makes the criterion achievable. This is not a statement about a general relation between ratings and cover; it applies only to the sort of ratings which will actually be bought.

In construction, which is described in the next section, this number will be the minimum GRPs which we allow to be bought in a period when we are on air. In evaluation, we can predict the percentage passing the cover criterion since we know from the schedule the number of GRPs in the period. The system for evaluation is called BAT as already noted. When cover is considered at the same time, the system is BAT + Cover.

Example of evaluation: flights vs. continuity with steady values and costs

I begin without any complications from variations in values and costs – they are assumed to be the same each week. This is not a real situation, it is an assumption to make sure that the findings are not influenced by these two factors.

Instead, the only variation comes from the assumptions about decay and diminishing returns. I investigate four situations: the combinations of a fast and a slow decay (one-week and six-week half-life), with steep and nearly linear response (steep response at $F = 80$ and nearly linear at $F = 20$).

I suppose the budget is enough to buy 2,000 GRPs. I have two ways I might allocate these. The first is in four flights of 500 GRPs, spread over four weeks at 125 GRPs a week. The second is continuous advertising at 40 GRPs a week, except for the last two weeks of the year.

I now have a way of evaluating the two sorts of schedule under each of the four conditions. My criterion is the effectiveness of the schedule as defined above, and my objective is to see which is the more efficient. I show the results in the table below, giving the effectiveness of the worse lay-down as a percentage of the effectiveness of the better.

	Half-life one week	Half-life six weeks
F = 80 (steep response)	Continuous	Continuous
	Flights = 70%	Flights = 99%
F = 20 (nearly linear)	Continuous	Continuous
	Flights = 96%	Flights = 96%

The main conclusion is clear. Under these artificial conditions, continuity is always the best policy, but there is little difference in the effectiveness of flighting – except in one case. If the half-life is short, and diminishing returns are steep, it is disastrous to flight. We lose 30 per cent in effectiveness.

In the other cases, flighting is much closer in effectiveness than you might expect – we lose a maximum of four per cent. This is an example of a general finding: provided you get the same number of total OTS (as we do in this case), differences in scheduling cause less variation in effectiveness than intuition suggests.

Another conclusion has to be relief that a clear answer is reached. Obviously the example is over-simple, not only in the artificial conditions, but because it looks at only one alternative to continuity and at only two half-lives and two rates of diminishing returns. A bigger table, covering more situations, would allow a more careful analysis about where the differences start to be serious. But the advantage of having a model is obvious. What could have been – and often has been – an inconclusive debate, now has a resolution.

Next, we look at this case history as an example of the relationship between scheduling and cover. Take the OTS distribution over any actual four weeks we are on air. This depends on buying details – channels and programmes – but here are some examples of the covers we are likely to get. The first column is for bursts, the second for continuous.

Cover	500 GRPs	160 GRPs
1+	76	56
2+	61	31
3+	51	17
4+	42	10

If we look for high cover when we are on air, say 60 per cent at 2+, we have to concentrate our advertising; bursts of 500 ratings in four weeks are necessary.

Be careful that such a criterion is really necessary. Over a longer period, like the whole campaign, cover will not be so different between the two schedules.

Example of evaluation: one week on, one off, etc. with steady values and costs

This example is also run without any complications from variations in values and costs – they are assumed again to be the same each week. Instead of the broad strategies evaluated in the above example, I look at a tactical question often asked. I compare a continuous schedule with its close flighting cousins. What difference does it make to be on air one week and off the next? Or, on for two weeks and off for two? Or, for three?

I set up four situations again: the combinations of very fast and less fast decay (this time half a week and two weeks half-life), with steep and nearly linear response (again steep response at $F = 80$ and nearly linear at $F = 20$). The budget is enough for 360 ratings, so 12 weeks at 30 ratings a week is the continuous schedule.

For each case I call the effectiveness of this continuous schedule 100, and I compare the effectiveness of the alternatives.

	1 on, 1 off	*2 on, 2 off*	*3 on, 3 off*
HL ½, F=80	89	85	84
HL ½, F=20	98	98	97
HL 2, F=80	100	98	96
HL 2, F=20	100	100	99

The table could be continued for longer half-lives, but the entries would soon all be 100, in other words, when decay is slow, the effectiveness of all these patterns of spending is much the same. The reason is clear – with a long half-life, adstock is maintained at a high level across the gaps in the schedule. The steepness of diminishing returns is not critical when decay is slow.

It is again only at very short half-lives and with steep diminishing returns that these schedules will be markedly worse in effectiveness than a continuous schedule. From calculations not shown here, I find that the half-life has to be one week or less, and F has to be 50 or more, for bursts to be much worse than the continuous schedule. The big drop in effectiveness is then due to having *any* gaps at all. Gaps of two or three weeks are not much worse than one week.

Much of the anxiety about choosing between these sorts of flights is wasted effort – it simply does not matter. Again, we feel relief that such a clear answer can be given.

Realistic values and costs

The findings just quoted were under conditions which made them as prominent as possible – when values and costs were constant. This is quite artificial. What is the effect of allowing for normal conditions?

To answer this question with a practical example, I take an example of values and costs which favours January, August and December. From January, the next two months see a rise in costs. The second quarter has high costs and Values/Costs are low throughout. It will make a difference whether I place the 12 weeks of continuous advertising in the first or second quarter. I therefore compare the schedules in both of these quarters, starting either in week 1 or in week 14.

Previously, total GRPs were 360 for all the schedules. Now, the total varies slightly with the schedules within the quarters, but the big difference is whether I use the first quarter (averaging 408 GRPs) or the second (313 GRPs).

I make the same comparison as before, with the continuous schedule. Indexing the other schedules on this, I now see some variety, but the picture is broadly the same. For example, for the key case of the half-life at half a week, and F = 80:

	1 on, 1 off	2 on, 2 off	3 on, 3 off
Quarter 1	88	84	83
Quarter 2	91	87	86

This is consistent with the first row of the table above; the same is true for the other rows. The conclusion suggested is that under real conditions, most of the time (there will always be exceptions), it is only at very short half-lives (one week or less) and with rather steep diminishing returns (F = 50 or more) that small gaps in the schedules (which have the same spend overall) lead to markedly worse effectiveness than a continuous schedule.

This comparison was made within a fixed period of 12 weeks. How do the schedules compare across the first and second quarters? We already know the first has 30 per cent more ratings. How about effectiveness? The following table compares the effectiveness of the alternatives placed in the first quarter, compared with the second:

	Effectiveness of Q1 schedule, indexed on Q2
HL 1/2, F=80	115
HL 1/2, F=20	123
HL 2, F=80	120
HL 2, F=20	125

We do not get as much improvement in effectiveness as we did in GRPs, especially for steep diminishing returns. This is because the additional GRPs do not pay off so well. But by moving to better Value/Cost time, we gain a very useful 15 to 25 per cent in effectiveness.

Thus the summary for this section, building also on general experience, is:
- pay attention to Values/Costs,
- increasing total ratings produces returns in effectiveness, especially for low F,
- small differences in schedule patterns (weeks on and off) are not important, except for very short half-lives and steeply diminishing returns, when continuity is recommended.

IMPROVEMENT

The way to improve a given schedule is similar to the evaluation of individual weeks, using the full model as at the end of Chapter 5. The difference is that I start with the existing schedule, instead of a blank sheet. I again evaluate the effect of adding GRPs in each week.

The result is that I have a number showing the increase in effectiveness for additional spend in each week. These numbers are now standardised: the average is now subtracted from each of them, to create an 'improvement index'. In a week where this is large and positive, added GRPs give a good return. Where the index is negative, especially large and negative, and if we have some GRPs there, we do least harm by taking some GRPs away (the slope of the relationship will apply to subtraction as well as addition). I therefore pay attention to weeks with a high positive index (which are asking for additions), and to weeks with a large negative index (where I can remove ratings, if I already have some in the schedule).

It would be possible to automate the process of improvement, but as I deal with the subject of a mechanical construction system next anyway, I have not done so here. Instead, I add manually in the weeks indicated and subtract where this seems sensible. Because the budget is fixed, I have to re-calculate the final GRPs, keeping the proportions as I have decided.

An example makes this clear.

In the section above, I concluded that continuous advertising starting in week 1 was the best of the alternatives considered, but not by much when the half-life was two weeks. This buys 404 GRPs, and its effectiveness, indexed on a continuous schedule throughout the year, is 104. I say 'best' when it was compared with small gaps in the schedule, and against similar patterns in quarter 2.

I now take an in-between value of F, at 50, and allow myself to improve effectiveness by any pattern of schedule at any time of year.

Running the improvement process described above gives indices falling into four clearly relevant groups:
– weeks 1 to 4, positive but small
– weeks 5 to 12, negative
– weeks 27 to 35, positive
– weeks 48 to 52, positive and large.
A sensible reaction to this information is first to cut GRPs in weeks 5 to 12, where the costs are rising and we already have a small effect from the first four weeks. Then to reinvest in weeks 27 to 35 and 48 to 52. In fact, the indices indicate specifically weeks 32 to 35 and 48 to 51. This buys more GRPs than the initial schedule: 430. It also raises the effectiveness considerably, to 113.

Further attempts to improve the second schedule show that this is hard to do. No further small changes got any major gains. Once more, it is not the fine detail which matters, but the big movement to better Value/Cost weeks.

CONSTRUCTION
What is 'hill-climbing'?

To explain hill-climbing, remember that the decision we are making is about allocating the money in the budget into 52 boxes – the weeks of the year. Further (and this is also explained below), suppose we have a 'unit' of expenditure. For the sake of argument (and this is not the actual unit used later), take one-hundredth of the budget as the unit.

Then we spend the budget in 100 individual decisions. The first decision is, in which week do we spend the first unit, or one-hundredth of the budget?

In order to decide, we look separately at each of the 52 alternatives. If we were to spend it in week 1, we would have a schedule (one-hundredth of the budget will buy so many ratings in week 1). This schedule can be evaluated: we calculate its effectiveness.

Then we consider the possibility of spending a unit in week 2. The unit in week 1 is eliminated – instead we have advertising in week 2 only. We calculate the effectiveness of this schedule.

Next, what about spending only in week 3? Only in week 4? And so on.

By the last week we have examined 52 alternative choices, all of which have been evaluated. Which step should we take? The answer is, the one with the largest effect – the steepest increase in effectiveness.

Having taken one step, we decide about the next, repeating the same evaluation of spending a second unit in each of the 52 weeks. This time, the unit already in place in the week selected in the first step remains there. Because this unit produces adstock over subsequent weeks, the evaluation of the result of each alternative is different from the calculation we did last time. The question is the same: which unit added to the existing schedule provides the steepest increase in total effectiveness?

You may imagine a large chess board, of 52 squares by 52. One side is labelled 'Week to choose first' and the other 'Week to choose second'. There are 52^2 or 2,704 squares in all, for just these two decisions. On each square, imagine a little tower, whose height equals the effectiveness of this schedule (when just two units have been spent). Looking at the board now, you see a mountain range. Where is the highest point?

Now we take not two steps, but 100, in this way. Each time we choose the steepest ascent, or greatest addition to the effectiveness of the schedule. We hope we have reached the summit of the hill on a very large chess board indeed, in 100 dimensions, with 52^{100} alternatives.

Strictly, it is the highest or best of the alternatives only if the terrain is 'well behaved'. There are some hill-climbing problems in which the path can start off on the steepest route only to miss some higher summit at the end which should have been approached in a more roundabout way. I assume this is not the case for most schedules, and this is why I said above a 'very good and often optimum' solution.

The practical solution

The hill-climbing principle is followed much as described above. The main difference is in the size of the steps, which were a constant amount of money. In practice, there are going to be two different sizes of step, the first determined by the minimum GRPs to buy, if the week is used at all.

In both cases, the step is now a certain number of ratings, not money. The description of hill-climbing given above was in steps of one-hundredth of the budget just for simplicity of explanation.

From the cover criterion set, we determine the minimum number of ratings per week required. This may be done on the advice of the buyer, or using a cover guide suitably adjusted for the special circumstances of the campaign being planned.

If the reporting period is longer than a week, there are complications, not dealt with here, in ensuring the conditions are met over the whole period. The point is that some *minimum* number of ratings is set, for times when we are on air at all.

Thus, when the week considered has no ratings already, the size of the step, if we take it, has to be this minimum number of ratings.

The second size of step is a purely practical choice: what is the fineness of detail required? This affects how long the computer run will last. A short step (say two or three ratings) means the final solution may have many different ratings for each week bought, since the ratings at this point are the sum of many possible small amounts; the run may also take some time (minutes rather than seconds, though this is a trivial disadvantage).

There is actually little point in the plan being too detailed, distinguishing say between 43 and 46 ratings in a particular week – no one can buy to this precision and plans are not written this way. A longer step means weeks will have only a few possible numbers of ratings and the run will be faster. We cannot make the step too big, or the process will not be very efficient. Steps of five at least, or ten, or 20 GRPs, are more normal.

Other practical considerations

The program also needs some routine inputs – the budget size is the most obvious.

It has to allow for certain weeks to have pre-allotted ratings. It has to stop using a week when ratings there have reached the maximum chosen.

At each step, the amount spent in buying the ratings has to be added to the running total, and the process stops when the budget has been exceeded. A way to spend the budget exactly is needed.

A record of the steps taken has to be kept – what was spent, how many GRPs were bought in which week and what is the effectiveness of the

Steps	Cumulative adspend	Cumulative GRPs	Effect so far	Week used
	0		0	
1	61,528	50	2	49
2	119,373	100	4	4
3	181,563	150	5	32
4	243,213	200	7	8
5	305,403	250	9	35
6	366,931	300	10	52
7	436,390	350	12	27
8	498,040	400	13	6
9	567,499	450	15	29
10	640,934	500	17	12
11	702,462	550	18	48
12	760,307	600	20	2
13	822,497	650	21	3
14	902,746	700	23	22
15	964,274	750	24	51
16	1,045,424	800	26	16
17	1,070,084	820	26	8

schedule to date. This is for several reasons. It is of interest to see how the effectiveness of the schedule grows as more money is spent. Is the effect of diminishing returns such that the last part of the money spent is hardly worthwhile? Also, we see which ratings were added first, and so are 'banker' weeks where we should retain expenditure at all costs, and which ratings were added last, and so can be lost if the budget is cut.

Since the best weeks were added first, the growth in effectiveness is faster then, both against spend and against GRPs, than towards the end of construction. When plotted, effectiveness is a convex curve. You might expect the rate of diminishing returns to be similar to the one assumed for adstock itself, as input for the construction. It is actually not as steep. This is because, for a single week, effectiveness would indeed improve in much the same way as for adstock. But the process is continually hunting for, and finding, better buys than repeating advertising in the same week.

Example of the steps taken

Table 7.1. Example of the first steps taken in a schedule construction
In Table 7.1, the first 17 steps are shown, for an actual schedule construction with F = 80 and with £7 million to spend. The best time for the first step was week 49. £61,528 was spent for the 50 ratings which were the minimum if a week was used at all. The second week, number 4, was a little cheaper: £57,845 was spent, making the total to date £119,373.

In this way the program initially picked 16 separate weeks in turn. Some were close to each other (weeks 48, 49, 51 and 52), others were isolated. It was not until step 17 that a week was chosen for a second time: number 8, when only 20 ratings were added as this was the size of subsequent steps. By then 15 per cent of the budget had been spent, but 26 per cent of the effect of a standard schedule at £7 million had been achieved.

This faster growth at the start, or higher efficiency per pound spent, is shown in Figure 7.1: the convexity on the left is clear. But even at the end, on the right, effectiveness is still growing well. The budget for the run had actually been set larger than the likely real spend. This was because the system was being used not only to suggest the schedule, but to comment on whether the last £1 million or so was worthwhile. In the event, effectiveness was not flattening off much and the larger spend looked sensible.

Two half-lives

The way in which a schedule is constructed when there are two half-lives to consider is finally dealt with. There are two methods.

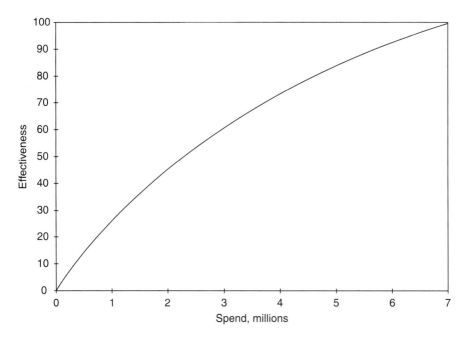

Figure 7.1 Example of schedule construction: how effectiveness grows

One method works in two stages. The proportion of the budget to be spent behind the more important half-life is used first to construct part of the schedule. These are then treated as obligatory ratings when the rest of the budget is spent, this time using the second half-life as the criterion. The advantage is that we see which parts of the schedule were priority for each half-life.

The other method is to evaluate each step by a suitably weighted combination of the half-lives chosen.

Using SWriter™ in a real example

This example was run for a medical product in Australia. Advertising was to start in week 6, with a minimum of 100 target ratings. We had $300,000 to spend, enough to buy about 500 more ratings at an average cost. Only half of the year (week 1–26) was to be planned. Values/Costs are plotted in Figure 7.2: note how they decline from week 6 to week 26.

So much for the environment. What sort of response did we look for from the campaign for this brand? The team completed a questionnaire to describe its expectations. The sort of scales used were explained in Chapter 5. From the answers, we derived the parameters for decay and diminishing returns. Also, we established that half the budget was to be spent on the long-term objective.

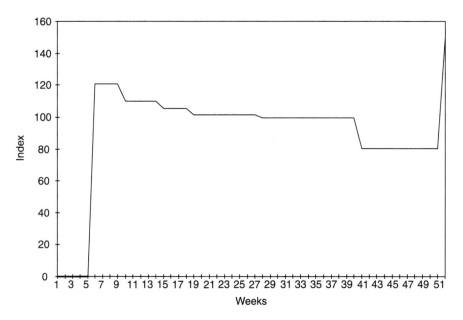

Figure 7.2 Values/Costs for Australian example

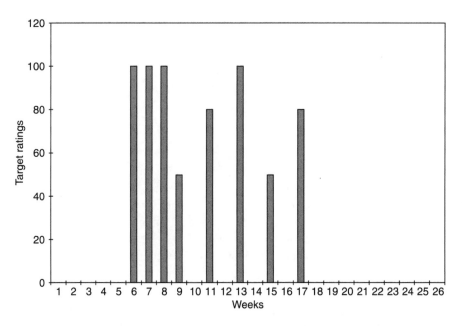

Figure 7.3 Recommended schedule for Australian example

The cover criterion was used to set the minimum rating when on air: 60 target ratings. Because there are few ratings to allocate, the maximum in any week was set at 100.

The first run of SWriter™ was carried out with the long-term parameters and in steps of ten ratings. It added 100 ratings to weeks 7 and 8. The money ran out while it was spending on week 9. With a long half-life, and lowest costs in these weeks, the program is building up adstock by spending as early as possible.

The second run took these ratings as obligatory and used the short half-life. The ratings still cluster early in the 20 weeks allowed, but are now more spread out. The final, recommended schedule is given in Figure 7.3.

How effective is this recommendation, compared with others we might have bought? The only comparison given here is with advertising contin-uously over the 21 weeks. Because this alternative spent more in the later, more expensive weeks, fewer ratings were bought. The efficiencies of the two schedules are compared in the table opposite, where the continuous schedule is indexed at 100, for each of the half-lives. The overall comparison is also given.

	Recommended	*Continuous*
Target ratings	655	617
Effectiveness:		
at short half-life	106	100
at long half-life	119	100
overall	113	100

In the short-term evaluation, the improvement is almost all due to increasing the number of ratings bought. For the long term, it mattered more that the effects started earlier. This also contributed to the overall improvement, showing the advantage of thinking explicitly about the long term. In total, the difference was +13 per cent or worth about $40,000.

Changing the input

The way the recommended schedule changes as the input is altered depends too much on the individual situation to be described generally. An example demonstrates the calculations to show what happens in an individual case.

I choose an example with a large budget and rather flat values over the year, to show that there are quite big reactions to altering the input even in this situation.

Suppose the budget can afford about 3,500 GRPs in the year. This is about 70 GRPs a week, and I set this as the minimum when on air, to meet a stringent cover criterion. The half-life is one week and diminishing returns are steep: F = 80. In these circumstances, you would expect a continuous schedule – unless values and costs were quite variable.

The first schedule was created without paying attention to costs – these were assumed to be uniform. Values did not alter much over the year – by about 10 per cent. Nevertheless, this variation was enough to concentrate the schedule into 44 weeks, as the table below shows.

When costs were allowed to vary over a normal range, concentration increased and only 37 weeks were bought.

Finally, I allowed two-fifths of the budget to be spent on longer term effects, allowing eight weeks for this half-life. The result was, naturally, to spend in even fewer weeks (28) where more ratings could be bought.

	Half-life	Weeks at 70 GRPs	Weeks over 70 GRPs	Total GRPs
Only values vary	1	34	10	3,500
Values and costs vary	1	19	18	3,400
Values and costs vary	60% at 1 40% at 8	19	9	3,700

This is an example of a general finding: schedules for large budgets tend towards flights as the underlying values and costs become more extreme, and as longer half-lives are allowed for. This is so, even when you would expect steep diminishing returns to favour continuity.

In this example, total GRPs are greatest for the last case, which also concentrates the schedule most.

Another example of changing the input

In this example, only the half-life and rate of diminishing returns were varied. The purpose is to demonstrate that the two inputs are distinct – we reach a different schedule when we change the rate of decay, keeping diminishing returns fixed. The reverse is also true.

The values of weeks in this example varied less than is usual: with a maximum indexed at 100 the minimum was 92. Costs varied over a normal range, the index was between 71 and 100. Two rates of decay were suggested, and diminishing returns were allowed at the two extremes: F at 20 per cent, so response was close to linear, and 80 per cent which is steep. The schedules are described by the number of weeks on air.

	Decay fast	*Decay slow*
F = 20	37	9
F = 80	51	15

Once more, with rapid decay and steep response, a continuous schedule is best. But slower decay, or flatter response, or both, cause the schedule to be run in different ways.

Example: supporting a promotion

In Chapter 1 we saw an example of advertising supporting a promotion. It is a classic of its kind – and this is a situation which often arises. For its link with British Airways, Sainsbury's bought 48 ratings in the first week of the promotion and 42 in the second week. Was this a wise decision? Should the ratings have been equal each week? Or, given that advertising has effects after its appearance, should advertising have started earlier? Was the second week necessary?

We have to guess the conditions which Sainsbury's assumed; from these assumptions we can comment on the alternatives.

Suppose the values allotted to the two weeks are equal, and that costs are like those assumed in Chapter 3 – rather steady in the last four weeks in September. We want an immediate effect, so a half-week half-life is assumed, or at the most a single week.

It is not worth thinking about any long-term effects here, though un-doubtedly such a promotion, well managed, does increase goodwill towards the company for some people for a long time. Because we have only a few ratings, it will not be very significant whether we choose the steep response curve appropriate to communicating a simple message (say, 80 per cent of maximum response at one OTS), or one rather flatter (50 per cent).

Under these conditions, I can calculate the optimum schedules. Ratings in the first and second weeks are as follows:

	Half-life = 1/2 week	*Half-life = 1 week*
F = 80	50, 40	90, 0
F = 50	60, 30	90, 0

With the most likely assumptions (half-week half-life and F = 80), the Sainsbury's solution was indeed indistinguishable from the best. If a little more repetition was thought desirable (F = 50), the first week might have been slightly upweighted. If the half-life was thought to be any longer (one week), all the money should be in the first week. The reason is that some ratings in the second week may appear after people have visited the store, so it is a less efficient time to advertise.

Sensitivity analysis

It is usually enough to find the optimum schedule for the conditions you have chosen. But we can return to the evaluation system and find out how efficiently the different solutions perform under the different assumptions that might be made. That is what we were actually doing in the evaluation example above which compared flights with continuity under conditions of steady values and costs. Now I do the same for the promotion example.

I can make my point by looking at only four assumptions, but in practice you might choose to make a larger table. The two schedules I examine are the two extremes. Below I show the ratings for the better schedule in each of four cases, with the amount by which the worse schedule performs under the same conditions.

	Half-life = 0.5 weeks	*Half-life = 1 week*
F = 80 (steep response)	50, 40	90, 0
	90, 0 = 89%	50, 40 = 87%
F = 20 (nearly linear)	90, 0	90, 0
	50, 40 = 98%	50, 40 = 83%

This shows the situation is quite sensitive. It is dangerous to choose the inappropriate solution in either direction. In Jones-Ephron conditions (short half-life, steep response – see Chapter 11) the 'flighting' schedule of 90, 0 loses 11 per cent in effectiveness. But if the half-life is a little longer, or diminishing returns are nearly linear, then the 90, 0 solution is better – and for the longer half-life it is a lot better.

The Italian example – concluded

In Figure 3.6 (p. 37) I showed the Value/Cost for an Italian grocery brand, and suggested that Value/Cost was so much higher in August that advertising would inevitably be in bursts. It turns out that this is not always so – it depends on the size of the budget, as well as on decay and diminishing returns.

The case most favourable to modified continuity is when the half-life is short (I take half a week) and diminishing returns are steep (F = 80). When I run with a budget which allows for about 2,600 ratings and a minimum rate

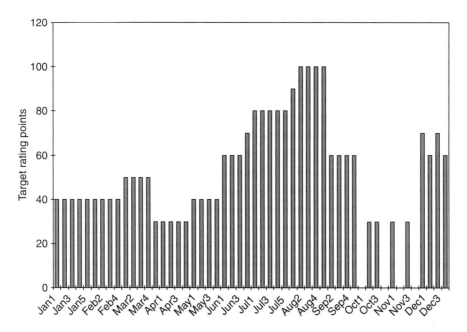

Figure 7.4 Recommended schedule for grocery brand, Italy: 2,630 TRPs

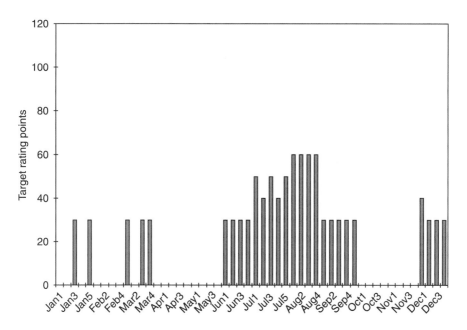

Figure 7.5 Recommended schedule for grocery brand, Italy: 1,020 TRPs

per week of 30, the resulting schedule is as shown in Figure 7.4. I am on air for 48 weeks – the exceptions are in October and November, where there are gaps of a single week. The shape is very like the Value/Cost curve, and indeed, the effectiveness of the schedule is very close to 100 – I might as well have copied the curve exactly.

It is better to do this than to be exactly continuous. To do this at 46 GRPs a week loses 200 GRPs in total and is 5 per cent less efficient.

However, when the budget is cut to one-third of this example, the shape of the best schedule changes. I can then choose to concentrate in better value time and buy 1,020 ratings. Thus for 33 per cent of the spend of the previous schedule, I get 40 per cent of the ratings. The schedule is now 6 per cent more efficient than one which follows Value/Cost. The stress on June to September is now very marked, as Figure 7.5 shows.

This is an example of one of the few advantages the small advertiser has – because of his flexibility he can buy more efficiently, though it may well be at a disadvantage in average cost for the weeks on air, because he may not be able to make the same deals. The large advertiser has to be near-average (within his dealing advantage) simply because his size leaves him little choice.

It is, of course, the actual efficiencies which matter, not the deals comparison. Unfortunately, the tendency of media controllers is to look at savings on deals first, rather than true effectiveness. They would say the large advertiser bought better, even when the small advertiser is, for his size, more efficient.

Realism

SWriter™ is a very powerful machine, but the hill it is climbing may have been mapped imprecisely – the parameters may have been badly chosen, the operating rules might not have foreseen every eventuality. So the machine may find a position which is outside our experience, or contradicts common sense for a very small theoretical gain. For example, if we enter a long half-life and flat diminishing returns, and no other restrictions, we are likely to get very few weeks used, with large numbers of ratings. It is hard to see all such possibilities before the run.

Statisticians are trained to remember, 'Your optimum only is bonum for the data you've fitted it to', as Tom Corlett put it.[2]

We meet the same problem more clearly in the next chapter. There the allocation is across different regions. When the solution suggested is that an important region gets no advertising, it is easy to see that something has gone awry. It is the same defect – a small alteration in a parameter has taken us into unexplored territory. The result is that the optimiser has chosen an apparent, probably small and certainly unsafe advantage which no human would trust.

Everyone sees that the important region must not be left out. The scheduling problem is harder, because our intuition about the right sort of solution is weaker. The continued debate about flighting versus continuity demonstrates that we do not easily see the right sort of thing to do.

Would we be wise to trust ourselves to a doctor in this way, when he may turn out to be Dr Jekyll or Dr Frankenstein? No, this would not be prudent. We cannot be sure of the assumptions or that the solution will always conform to what is thought practical.

But it would also be wrong to turn our backs on a potential ally. The solution is optimum – for some conditions. It is the conditions which need adjustment, rather than rejecting the machine. It needs tuning and direction, that is all.

My recommendation, as with all models, is first to ensure that you can quickly get alternatives and are not stuck with a single 'best'. Second, to inspect output critically, and to be ready to reject it if it offends common sense. Turn the screw a bit and try again. The machine can give another optimum, and next time the conditions it is using may be more appropriate.

Two quick examples of common-sense adjustment will now be given. The first is when the process suggests a small number of ratings in a week isolated from the rest of the schedule. This can happen when the budget is too small to build a reasonable number of ratings, at a period which is at a higher Value/Cost than other times which might be used. Buyers would reject such parts of a schedule as difficult to justify and uneconomic to buy and administer. In these cases, add the money to periods already chosen, ignoring the fact that diminishing returns make them a little less efficient: the overall harm to the schedule will be negligible.

The second sort of example is in details too fine for the weekly unit used here to cover, such as preference for individual days or programmes. Similarly, there is evidence quoted in Chapter 12 that a very concentrated set of exposures may have a benefit above that of the normal distribution of ratings during the week. Again, the calculated recommendation may require manual or within-week adjustment.

Detailed example: controlling the machine

Now I consider the circumstances which might have led to the Persil Wash-up Liquid schedule in Chapter 1. The variations in Value/Cost are typical. There is not enough money to be continuous at the sort of GRP levels I have decided are necessary for the cover criterion we want. That is, I know that the solution should be flights, but I do not know when or how many.

In this example, I take quite a long half-life – six weeks – and a steep rate of diminishing returns, F = 80. The budget is enough to buy 585 GRPs, if I spread it over the year so that GRPs are in proportion to Value/Cost. This averages only 11 GRPs a week.

Three approaches are described and compared. The first is using evaluation techniques. The second is to construct an 'optimum' schedule and then modify it, again using evaluation and improvement methods. Finally, I use the facility of a maximum limit.

1. I find out that if I actually bought 11 GRPs every week I would lose 2 per cent in effectiveness, compared with ratings in proportion to Value/Cost. This is mainly because the 585 GRPs of the standard schedule fell to 576 as I put money into higher-cost weeks.

Starting from this continuous schedule I can cut the worst Value/Cost weeks and so raise my effectiveness. By this process I can pick 31 weeks in each of which I buy 21 GRPs. I have now got total ratings up to 642, and effectiveness usefully up to 109. This might well be the sort of 'modified continuity' schedule I decide to buy.

2. But can I do better than this? Is it right to go for a low level of advertising under these conditions? The question is answered by constructing the optimum schedule, first without any maximum rating limit. This concentrates advertising into only five weeks, one of which gets 340 GRPs. The result is an amazing improvement in the GRP total, to 711, and in effectiveness, to 115.

Few planners would run this hypothetical schedule. It follows from the conditions laid down, but it had no maximum GRP limit, nor did it pay attention to the sort of cover criterion normally required – in one week it allocates only 25 GRPs. I could therefore modify this suggestion by spreading the GRPs round the extreme peaks suggested. But this time I am starting from a position of strength. Instead of assuming that continuity of some sort is vital, subject to a minimum level of GRPs, I know where concentration is required. Can I explore round the suggested peaks and spread the GRPs to make the schedule more acceptable without losing too much effectiveness?

The answer is that I can. Once more we see that some changes in scheduling, which intuition says will be serious, actually differ little in effectiveness. It is the broad shape of the schedule and its strategy which matters, more than the detail or tactics.

So I use the improvement and evaluation systems to make common-sense judgments about where to spread the GRPs which the optimum system has selected. In ten minutes and three rounds of adjustment I have an acceptable compromise between the best or most effective times to be on air and a more normal rate of flighting. I finish with five flights, totalling 13 weeks on air, and GRP rates per week between 46 and 63. I buy 678 GRPs and get an effectiveness of 112.

3. Finally, I can construct a schedule subject to a maximum limit for ratings each week. It turns out that this also has an effectiveness of 112, for 15 weeks on air, and ratings of between 55 and 45.

The situation is summarised as follows:

	Weeks on air	Min/max GRPs	Effectiveness
Continuous	52	11 / 11	98
Modified continuous	31	21 / 21	109
'Optimum'	5	25 / 341	115
Modified optimum	13	46 / 63	112
Optimum with maximum	15	55 / 45	112

It is evident that modifying the continuous strategy is a big improvement. But it is still better to start from the optimum and modify that, or to set a maximum for ratings per week and construct a schedule under these conditions.

Conclusions

This chapter describes a model which represents how advertising affects sales. The model has been found to be realistic in many conditions.

The planner about to write a schedule can describe the environment and objectives for the brand and the campaign. This description can be turned into input for the model.

A process using the model with appropriate input can help the planner in two important ways. First, it can evaluate alternatives, showing whether different schedules have very different sales-effectiveness. Second, it can make its own suggestion.

This process has been applied to a variety of situations and schedules. We learn that in some circumstances, the differences between schedules are unimportant: we need not be much concerned about such differences. Disputes about what is best to do are then easily resolved.

In other circumstances, sales-effectiveness can be markedly improved. The schedule recommended by the process, or one close to it, clearly gives a better return on investment.

A final summary:
- The appropriate schedule depends on the particular circumstances, there is no single solution.
- There is a method of reaching the relevant solution and it can markedly raise the effectiveness of the advertising.

8   Where to advertise?

Introduction

The subject here is another allocation problem. It occurs when there are different regions where we may buy television separately, like markets in the US, or TV regions in the UK. This is not possible in some countries, or for some channels, where TV is bought nationally. In such cases, skip this chapter. For those interested, this is a rapid review of the possibilities. The chapter is technical but short.

An alternative is that countries themselves may be the regions; it is an allocation over a continent, or even global. This is not followed up here, though some of the ideas do apply. The reason this is different is because larger issues are raised. The nature of category itself, the brand situation, distribution, costs and profitability – all these may vary across countries. The same can be true across markets in the US, and when such diversity reaches a certain level, strategic considerations outweigh simple comparisons of advertising weight and cover.

So from now on I assume a uniform strategy, with variations in regional values to the advertiser, and different costs, but no more.

There is still a big difference between this allocation, and the spread over time. Increasing the spend in one *region* affects others only because it takes money from them. This is a complication we can cope with straight-forwardly. But increasing the spend in one *week* not only takes money from others, it creates adstock which alters the response in later weeks. That is why Chapter 7 was more complex than this one.

The two decisions overlap. When you give more money to one region, so that more television ratings can be bought there, you may alter the kind of schedule you buy. For example, you may be able to afford an additional burst; for a near-continuous schedule, you might increase the number of weeks on air.

There are three approaches. First, you allocate the budget *to* regions and then schedule *within* regions. Or, you decide on a typical schedule and modify it in some regions. Finally, you can do both jobs together.

Allocation across two regions

Suppose that we can buy television advertising time on stations whose audiences are geographically separate. This separation may not be absolute – there can, in practice, be overlap areas, but this is not taken into account here.

As you were reminded in Chapter 2, these regions are likely to be of different sizes (the numbers in the target audience who can be reached by the station) and to have different costs. Northland and Southshire contained respectively 1,500 and 721,000 housewives. Their average costs in 1997 for 1,000 OTS on homemakers were £7.10 and £8.17. Another way of giving the costs is how much it takes to buy 100 ratings. For Northland, for example, 100 ratings means 1,500,000 impacts. This costs £10,657 (1,500 times £7.10). In Southshire, 100 ratings cost £5,894.

People in different regions are likely to be of different values to the advertiser, as we saw in Chapter 2. I now mean in addition to their sizes and their general economic health. If I have no sales outlets in a region, there is little point in advertising there. But if a new product has done particularly well in a region, and I decide to support success, a member of the target audience there has above-average value.

Are these three characteristics – costs, the number in the target audience and the value of a member of that audience – enough information on which to base a regional allocation? Indeed they are.

Having introduced the ideas, it is time to take a more systematic approach. There are plenty of different aids for the allocation of a budget over regions, in fact the main difficulty is choosing between them. So I start with a description of the sorts of help available.

Simple formulae

Some methods are so simple they are hardly thought of as formulae, but that is how they should be applied. 'Equal impacts' is an example, when each region gets the same number of ratings. 'In proportion to sales' is another, when ratings – or budget – are allocated in the same ratio as our brand's current sales.

Diminishing returns

Just as there are diminishing returns to increasing ratings during a single week, there are diminishing returns to increasing the ratings in a region. We have to decide how steep the relation is, between ratings and response. In this application too, the steeper the curve, the more likely we are to approach a flat allocation, or equal ratings across regions.

This 'flexible' method starts by choosing a parameter, which describes the steepness of diminishing returns. With this parameter, there is a single best allocation,[1] one which maximises total sales.

Modify the current allocation

Both of those methods started from scratch – only the facts about costs, population and so on. In contrast, we can start from the existing allocation, and look at ways to improve it.

Allocate over time and regions

All these methods treat the regional question separately from scheduling. But really the two are connected. If a region gets a lot more money, we may schedule there differently, perhaps even shifting from flighting to continuity in some cases, simply because we could not afford continuity before.

Of course, we can make the decisions in sequence, but another approach is to generalise the hill-climbing approach to scheduling. In the last chapter the method was described as putting money into 52 cells, one for each week. But suppose we have ten regions to cover: we can think of 520 cells (the year over each region). At each step the method evaluates all the weeks in each of the regions, instead of only 52 weeks in total. It picks the most sales-effective week and region, and continues to do so until the budget is exhausted.

Review of the four methods

Having defined the four approaches, I now comment on each of them. For interested readers, there is more about the first three in another publication,[2] and in the notes.

Formulae methods

For an 'equal impacts' allocation between Northland and Southshire we need no more than we already know. In the notes we see the calculation which gives 603 ratings in both regions when the budget is £100,000.

In order to take the 'values' of the regions into account we need to know more. There are various criteria which might be used: how well the category is doing in the regions, or how well the brand does, since supporting success is a common strategy. The profit we make on a sale in each region might also have to be used.

Suppose, for example, we decide that the relative values of a shopper in the two regions are 90 and 130 (more in the notes). This is exactly the same approach as giving values to weeks when we were scheduling. Then we can make the ratings bought fall in the same proportion: 521 and 752. Or, we can ignore costs, and split the budget in proportion to the population size times the value of an individual (this might be equivalent to the brand's current sales). The resulting ratings are similar in this case: 553 and 694.

These allocations split the budget in the following ways:

	Northland, £	Southshire, £
Equal impacts	64,379	35,621
Ratings in proportion to value of an individual		
	55,580	44,420
Budget in proportion to population x value of an individual		
	59,022	40,978

In this case the difference between the last two allocations is not likely to make a difference to the type of schedule bought, but between the first two the schedule might well change.

Diminishing returns

We need to fix a parameter to determine this allocation. When d is near zero, we get close to the equal impacts solution. As d increases towards its maximum, which is one, the regions with better Value/Cost receive more and more money and ratings. In this case it is Southshire, since the value of a shopper here is 44% better, while costs are only 15% higher. Each allocation is the most efficient for this particular value of the parameter.

Examples of two solutions in this case are given:

	Northland budget, £	Northland ratings	Southshire budget, £	Southshire ratings
$d = 0.90$	56,187	526	43,813	742
$d = 0.95$	47,553	446	52,447	888

Modify the current allocation

These calculations need more data. As well as the sales rate in each region we need to know the previous rate of advertising. The method moves advertising rates up in some regions, down in others, for the year to come. The principle is that advertising has an effect on sales, and the adjustments are made so that, for a fixed total spend, total sales are maximised.

Again a parameter is needed. This time it is the sales elasticity of the advertising spend, written E. Some results from the calculation are:

Elasticity, E	Northland budget, £	Northland GRPs	Southshire budget, £	Southshire GRPs
0.1	50,845	476	49,155	832
0.5	57,546	539	42,454	719
0.7	67,034	628	32,966	558

The method again provides a range of allocations. For both the flexible methods I usually choose one which is not too extreme, for the same reasons as given at the end of Chapter 7.

Allocate over time and regions

Of the various ways to make this decision, I normally recommend the following. Use the diminishing returns allocation to study how far your budget will stretch when good Value/Cost regions are rewarded. Try various values of the parameter d, concentrating on the lowest and the highest ratings suggested. A common practical rule for large budgets is that ratings in the highest region should be no more than twice those in the lowest. Consider the types of schedule, the covers and frequencies you are likely to get, especially at the low values.

The next step is to simplify the results of the calculation. Some regions may be dropped completely. Others may be grouped, so that we have high-priority and low-priority regions, and in each group we have similar ratings.

Finally, plan within regions.

Do diminishing returns (within a week) apply across regions?

In the formula method of allocation across regions, the parameter d controls how much goes to the best region (judged by value and cost). When d is near 1, repetition is acceptable; the best region gets a large proportion of the budget and high GRPs.

Does the parameter for diminishing returns within a week (F or the percentage of maximum response at the rate of one OTS a week) imply that the same should be used for d, across regions?

The answer, unexpectedly, is 'no'. The reason becomes clear when we refer to the previous chapter, about the way sales-effectiveness increases as more is spent. It was shown there that this relationship is flatter than the curve described by F. In Figure 7.1 (p. 91), with over 5,000 ratings a year and with $F = 80$, when a geometric curve was fitted, d turned out to be 0.992.

Part 2

Other solutions

It is our responsibility as scientists, knowing the great progress which comes from a satisfactory philosophy of ignorance... to teach how doubt is not to be feared, but welcomed and discussed.[1]

In this part of the book, I cover much of the same ground as before: the decay of advertising effects, diminishing returns, 'effective frequency' and the implications for scheduling. The difference is that I describe mostly the methods and conclusions of others. Some I disagree with, some I support. There may be ideas here which you previously found convincing, but I now persuade you otherwise. You will make up your own mind.

Decades of confusion are being left behind, but many of the old views are still around. These are all based on various ideas about how advertising works. Researchers who concentrate on this often pay scant attention to its specific applications. People who write TV schedules have often picked up, uncritically, what they believe researchers said. It is often they, and not the original researcher, who apply the concepts to media decisions. By tracing where the ideas came from, and how far the evidence supports them, you will find it easier to decide which to follow.

The debate has covered some of the most vital subjects in media and advertising research and the implications go far beyond scheduling.

The ideas do not emerge out of darkness, they are put forward by individuals. This is not an abstract debate, but the interaction of personalities. I have stressed this here because it makes the subject easier to understand and, I hope, more interesting.

The next four chapters feature in turn Timothy Joyce, Colin McDonald, Mike Naples, John Philip Jones, Walter Reichel, Erwin Ephron and Andrew Roberts. Of course there are many others whose input has been important, and who also feature below, but the main thread of the argument can be traced through these seven.

This part is also an historical review and the chapters are arranged roughly by decades: I start in the 1960s and earlier (Chapter 9), continue with the 1970s and 1980s (Chapter 10), and divide the 1990s into an early period (Chapter 11) and late (Chapter 12).

Darwin and TV schedules

It is a temptation which I cannot resist to compare the different *shapes* of schedules discussed in this book with *species* of animals or plants. Some are distinct: a single short burst is obviously different from uniform weight across the year. Others are like varieties, hard to tell apart, as Darwin noted: the uniform schedule merges into ratings in proportion to Values/Costs; in bursts, times allowed off air may be one week only, or two or three.

The environment in which some shapes flourish are certain budget sizes, certain values and costs. Within these, decay and diminishing returns are like genes which control how the shape develops. Shapes of schedule compete, they increase or become extinct; we have seen that continuity is currently growing at the expense of flighting. Some kind of selection is going on.

The reason for the analogy is that Darwin lists, in the first chapter of *The Origin of Species*, the conditions under which human selection produces the best results.

1. We need 'a high degree of variety' in our material; this is certainly true for us.
2. 'The most important point of all is that the animal or plant should be so highly useful to man, or so highly valued by him, that the closest attention should be paid to even the slightest deviation.' You would think this should apply to efficiency gains which can be achieved by relatively little application, but the subject has not been noted for 'close attention'. Nor has the logic of the arguments used been outstanding.
3. The breeder can select only by what is 'externally visible'. Here we fall down badly, since the advertising effect on sales has so seldom been reliably measured. A good schedule and a poor one are rarely seen to be so.
4. In Darwin's day, the 'laws governing heredity were quite unknown'. We have made advances in genetics since then. In scheduling, we try to use what we believe we know, about how advertising works, in order to write better schedules. We too seldom experiment to make the differences 'externally visible'.
5. 'A large number of individuals ... under favourable conditions of life' are necessary as a pool for the breeder to choose from. It is only major advertisers who have such a pool. However, we are able to see what our competitors are doing, and it strikes me as strange that so little attention is paid to their schedules and their results.
6. Free communication – the spreading of, and knowledge about, new sub-breeds – are conditions of success. But we often share information only reluctantly and rarely.

One of the purposes of this part of the book is to describe the beliefs and strategies of the different 'breeders' of schedules. What was it that 'caught the fancier's eye'?

My own prediction is that uncertainty about the right schedule will reduce. The last four decades have seen too many wild-goose chases. No longer should we have the swings of fashion to which this decision has been subjected. It will become clearer which species fits each particular habitat. Diversity should be seen as a sensible strategy, not a sign of failure. Darwin would have approved.

9 Single source – the early pioneers

The birth of single-source research

Until the 1960s, discussions about the effects of repeated exposures of advertising were largely academic. The 'response function' was rarely measured; the way time entered the definitions was unclear. The few pieces of research on the subject (for example, the Zielske work re-analysed in Chapters 4 and 5) were seized on eagerly.

A review[1] suggested that the effects of repetition were well fitted by the same curve I and others still use – the geometric formula in Chapter 5. So when the parameter F is high, 'Cover is very important indeed. Only the first impression on an individual counts' (Broadbent & Segnit 1967).

The choice of burst or of fairly evenly spaced advertising seemed at this time to follow no rules: a list of factors to bear in mind[2] was all there was on offer. It is not so different for too many people today.

There is only one way to measure directly the connection between a shopper's opportunities to see TV advertising, and her subsequent choice of brands; that is, to create a panel of shoppers whose TV exposure is measured. This sort of research is called single source – a single panel provides the data about an individual's viewing and her shopping. The story of its first appearance and use is relevant to many of today's questions.

The effects of advertising

In the 1960s J.Walter Thompson in London had a Research Committee whose purpose was to develop new ideas and new techniques. Its Secretary was Stephen King; Timothy Joyce was perhaps its most fruitful thinker.

On his first day at work, in 1958, Joyce was set one of the tasks which was to preoccupy much of his professional life: how to detect the effects of advertising. He designed a survey called the Advertising Planning Index. This measured what were accepted then as the scores which advertising was to influence: the image of the brand, attitudes towards it, intention to buy and so on.

The survey grew into a large and respected service. For several years it was one of BMRB's largest jobs. In 1962 it interviewed 7,000 people a month and earned 12 per cent of their revenue.[3] What was more, it span off other services and became a database which could be mined for generalities. Some[4] were surprising, for example, the discovery that instead of changes in attitude preceding increased sales, the opposite was often the case. Behaviour could be the first to change, and it was the new or more frequent buyers whose attitudes altered. Another lesson, and one which in the end doomed the survey, was that attitudes were rather stable; it hardly seemed worth paying for a service which produced similar results month after month.

A large part of the questionnaire was taken up by measurement of the media exposure of the informants. Joyce experimented with other ways to collect this information, including a leave-behind section which became a diary about reading and viewing which the shopper was asked to fill in. This information had its own uses and was welcomed by the media planners at JWT, since it was the first time they were able to see in detail how their targets were exposed to advertising. Eventually, purchasing questions were added to this diary. The first single-source data were being collected and Joyce was their parent.

It soon became clear that the single-source panel was an uneconomic way of collecting the data needed for what became their Target Group Index, launched in 1968, and which put my own attempt, the All-Media and Product Survey, out of business. A survey – albeit with a long questionnaire left for self-completion – was more efficient when media planning was the objective.

What to do with the single-source data they had collected? They agonised over these data for some time. Stephen King tells me that the committee members each took home the records of 30 shoppers and simply stared at the raw data. It was genuinely exciting to have this connection with the real world, instead of the aggregates which so often tried to represent it.

He suggested, to general astonishment, that perhaps advertising was more important as reassurance to existing buyers than in making converts. The analysis given later on shoppers switching between brands was the most powerful for some purposes, but to see evidence about its effect in retaining buyers was to him at least as significant.

He also saw the extreme difficulty of making sensible groups of the data: 'If you had 30 shoppers to look at,' he says, 'you saw 30 patterns.' It was a radical idea at the time that each shopper had a 'repertoire' of several brands, rather than one which they were loyal to. It was also unusual to follow through what a single shopper did. Normally, the situation was summarised one month, and then again in a later month. We then concluded that not much had changed (this is still a common view). Below the surface, the feet of the swan were paddling madly.

A new face

Colin McDonald moved at the age of 35 from the Market Research Department of Reckitts in Hull to BMRB. He worked first on the National Readership Survey. He was recognised as a thoughtful person who would be best used worrying away at a problem on his own. In 1968, Joyce suggested that McDonald worked with him on the single-source data. Joyce knew that there was more there than had been laid bare.

Funding was obtained from JWT and McDonald started, as others had done, by scrutinising the data. No computers were available and even punched cards were not used, as no one knew what analyses to do, or what patterns to look for.

For three product fields, huge spreadsheets were laboriously filled in: shoppers down the side, days along the top, purchases in blue ink, advertisements in red.

Joyce published an overview[5] of the methods of data collection which BMRB was experimenting with, including single source. This shows what the spreadsheets looked like. For his example with only 19 respondents and for three weeks, the picture is daunting! This was the first ever view of single-source data the world had seen. The analysis he was thinking about, and which later McDonald was to carry out, was not revealed. The only conclusion – and a very British one – is that a single-source diary is 'perhaps one of the things the industry should be thinking about'.

When it came to an advertising effect, McDonald knew, and Joyce reminded him, of the risk of what we now call Purchase/Viewing bias. He had read the paper[1] on response functions, published the year before, which emphasised the point. Heavy buyers of a brand may watch more TV and so see more ads. In his 1970 paper, he spells out the danger quite explicitly:

We must first make sure we avoid the spurious relationship between weight of buying the product and weight of viewing. ... A conventional cross-tabulation ... will not do.

He saw that a way to deal with this was to look, within each shopper, at brand choices of two types. A switch to our brand means first a purchase which was not our brand, then one which was our brand. A switch away from our brand is the reverse. 'Even if there are more switches into Persil among heavy viewers, there will be the same number of switches out of Persil among the same viewers', except at the beginning or end of these sequences. The point is that an analysis of switches overcomes the problem they were both worried about. McDonald sees it as 'achieving an experimental analysis of non-experimental data.' And, 'if one asks the right question one can often by-pass the failing of data-as-it-falls, not being a designed experiment.'

In his very first analysis,[6] which was of three product fields, he cunningly looked at sets of three successive purchases, by the same viewer, in which a repeat purchase was followed by a switch (A-A-B). He reasoned that if there were ad effects 'we might expect to find more OTS for A in the space or interval between the first two purchases (A-A) than between the second two (A-B), and we might expect to see the reverse for B.' The evidence was consistent with the hypothesis that there was an effect, and it was only after this that he attempted to generalise further and look at single intervals.

McDonald wrote about 'the universe of purchasing occasions'. That is, each shopping decision is an event which can be defined in various ways – what brand was bought, who bought it, what she bought before – and also what advertising was seen by this shopper previous to this occasion.

These seem to me his two major contributions – carrying out the within-person analyses and defining the universe of purchasing occasions. Media people saw the data, in particular about TV programmes, as a new description of how media reached people. Manufacturers saw it as a description of who bought what, and so it was a way of understanding their own brand. McDonald saw it as a mine of data about the effects of advertising.

The weak theory

Timothy Joyce used data from this panel and other sources to think through better than any of us what was really going on when shoppers saw advertisements. I heard him talk at Deauville in 1965, 'What do we know about how advertising works?' (the 1967 version is the one usually reprinted[7]). The phrase 'how advertising works' must have been used before, but for me it is associated with listening, open-mouthed, as he demolished many accepted ideas and put in their place a simpler, totally convincing structure.

He argued that the old view – advertising drove people through stages of awareness, belief and so on – should be replaced by a shopper-centred model. People use advertising as part of their view of the world. Their shopping priorities are about themselves and their families. Advertisers are not in charge; shopping is the most democratic of all activities. His approach was shared by Stephen King,[8] and is currently most publicised by the analyses of Andrew Ehrenberg[9] and by the more entertaining but equally serious ex-Chairman of JWT, Jeremy Bullmore.[10]

The McDonald findings

McDonald's paper outlining his first results did not appear until 1969, and a second was given in Barcelona[11] in 1970. His purpose was not primarily to help media planners, though he mentioned scheduling. He had a different objective – to show beyond doubt that advertising could have effects on sales.

Admittedly, these were only short-term advertising effects (one measure described below is about advertising seen in the four days before purchase). This was pointed out by JWT:[12] 'The effects of advertising are primarily cumulative and repetitive over a period of time. One would expect these effects to be least obvious over the short term.'

The sample was so small (from 255 housewives over 13 weeks) that no individual brand data were ever published – only aggregates over the brands. Only part of the data (about switches to and from our brand) was used for the analysis which made the most impact. But they were direct advertising effects on behaviour at a time when the industry view was that it was impossible to see them.

When I heard McDonald give his 1970 paper I shared the platform with him. My own paper was also about measuring ad effects. Our technique at the London Press Exchange used traditional questions in surveys about shoppers' understanding of how the brand (an insecticide strip called Vapona was our example) did its job. Our innovations improved on the traditional pair of surveys (before and after the campaign) by using different media (television and press) in an experimental design in four different regions. We added questions about habits of media exposure so that we could deduce how much advertising the informants were likely to have received.

It is by area testing that I tried, like so many at the time, to answer the question of post-campaign evaluation. The samples were large; there was no question of looking at individuals; the method worked for any type of advertised product – airlines, insurance and cars, as well as the groceries to which single source is currently restricted. I was so excited by this technique, which we had used on 30 brands by 1969, that I failed to see myself the potential of single source.

What did McDonald show?

McDonald has analysed the 1966 data in many different ways. He continues to use the various approaches on data today. They are all based on contingency tables which classify the shopping occasions of his informants in various ways.

He had 32,000 observations, when he had added up the pairs of purchases described below for all nine categories, each with several brands. Of these, nearly 20 per cent had some advertising (for the brand studied) seen by the shopper in the four days before purchase. The question is, did seeing advertising appear to have any connection with the choice of brand? He had pairs because he recorded which brand was bought at the previous purchase. So he took partly into account the important factor of different loyalties to the brand. He had four possibilities for the two occasions:

– didn't buy the brand either time, so likely to be loyal to some other brand,
– bought our brand last time and this time, so likely to be loyal to us,
– changed to the brand,
– changed away from it – both being disloyal acts to some brand.

In real life the first possibility is the most likely, since few brands have very large shares of market – for any shopper, she is most likely not to buy our brand. The other three groups were roughly of the same size, at about 15 per cent of all purchases.

To measure advertising pressure, he considered *two* sorts of interval before the purchase. He looked at all the days since the shopper's previous purchase in the category. In that case, opportunities to see the relevant commercial were counted 'in the purchase interval'. This number of days varies, since it is short for someone who buys frequently (a heavy shopper with many people to cater for, or who buys small sizes) but long for infrequent shoppers. This makes interpretation hard. He also looked within a fixed number of days before the purchase. This number varied from a single day, through four, to seven. Thus he was looking at 'propinquity' or closeness to purchase in a way which others like Reichel and Roberts have since repeated, and which Ephron has made popular.

As explained above, the most secure way to find some kind of advertising effect is to look only at the times the shopper switched to this brand or from it. The reason this is the preferred way is that there can be no contaminating influence *across* people (like having different brand loyalties, or watching more TV) which might influence the proportion of switches *to* the brand out of all switches.

If advertising has *no* effect, we must get the proportion of switches *to* the same as *from*, whether any advertising is seen or not. In fact, in his data McDonald found that, when a shopper had seen advertising for the brand in the four days before, then her share of switches was 50.5 per cent. When she had not, her share was 49.8 per cent. The ratio of these two numbers is 1.014. In other words, there is a short-term effect of advertising, and, with these definitions, it is that shoppers who switch are 1.4 per cent more likely to switch *to*, when they saw some advertising for the brand.

This does not sound earth-shaking, but at the time this sort of evidence was the first proof that short-term effects, for heavily advertised groceries, existed at all. Though the number is small, and the limitation to the short term and to switches is restrictive, the implications are important.

Is this a response function?

McDonald however went further. He divided the occasions into groups by the number of OTS for the brand the shopper had seen since the last purchase. When he looked at switches in this way, the results were as follows:

Opportunities to see	0	1	2	3	4 or more
Percentage of switches to the brand	50	47	54	53	54

The five figures in this simple table (and in a similar one where the interval was since the last purchase occasion) had worldwide effects, which is why this small study is so important. McDonald wrote, 'It may well pay to ensure (when scheduling) that the target population will see more than one OTS between purchases.' For nearly three decades this idea, shortened to 'Two OTS in the purchase interval', became a principle of media planning for many – and even a way of determining a budget (enough to buy two OTS in the purchase interval).

The response appears to be negative at one OTS, climbs at two OTS and then stays steady. No matter that this sum used only a quarter of the observations, ignoring the important 'loyal' people who bought us both times; no matter that because switches must average 50 per cent, one group at least must be below 50 per cent if others are above it (which is why we get the apparent negative effect); no matter that this was an average over different brands and that the interval used is one never available in schedule analyses. To the satisfaction of many schedulers, the 'effective frequency' had been 'proved' to be two. Media people are not too scrupulous about where their criteria come from.

A modern analysis

I now show another analysis[13] actually carried out later, on the whole data set. Instead of an analysis of switches, I give the brand shares in groups of occasions by the number of OTS before the purchase; the interval here is four days.

Opportunities to see	0	1	2	3	4 or more
Number of occasions	27,487	4,228	1,142	380	204
Brand share, %, indexed at 100 for 0 OTS	100	126	147	140	151

This time the number of observations is given, as well as the findings in the last line. To show the size of the sample is good manners – it allows the reader to form a view about the reliability of the results. The numbers are more than adequate to say that the brand share was about a quarter higher for the group with one OTS than for the group with none, and nearly twice this increase for the group with two OTS. But McDonald stops at 'four or more' – to break this group down further would be to risk unreliable brand shares.

The second row is also interesting in its own right. The great majority of occasions took place without any OTS for the brand in a period as short as four days before purchase. At three or more OTS we are down to 584 occasions, or under 2 per cent of the total. Very few shoppers are that heavily exposed to recent advertising. There is another reason for giving the figures, which I return to when I have commented on the last row.

Because we have the numbers of observations, we can group the data in other ways, since we are able to calculate the necessary weighted averages. For instance, we can deduce:

Opportunities to see	0	1	2 or more
Number of occasions	27,487	4,228	1,726
Brand share, %, indexed at 100 for 0 OTS	100	126	146

We can even make this table – and the purpose will be clear later:

Opportunities to see	0	1	Any OTS
Number of occasions	27,487	4,228	5,954
Brand share, %, indexed at 100 for 0 OTS	100	126	132

The results at one OTS come from so many observations that they outweigh the higher OTS in the last column headed 'Any OTS'. In fact they provide 71 per cent of the final cell, so there is a lot of double-counting in the last two cells. The table states that we get a result at only one OTS which is almost as high as for any number of OTS: plus 32 per cent is not that much above plus 25 per cent. This can be interpreted (wrongly) as, 'More than one OTS gives little additional effect'. The table above showed that the increase to two OTS or more nearly doubles the response at one OTS. Such are the perils of weighted averages!

Some later attempts at data collection

1. Joyce and McDonald co-operated in an American attempt to repeat and enlarge the original British single-source trial of the late 1960s. This took place ten years later, and was the result of an initiative by *Newsweek*. In 1977 the magazine published an advertisement in a series about media planning. The headline was 'We want to know what you want to know', and the advertising industry (from which the magazine wanted more business) was asked its priorities in research. One common answer was what the magazine hoped for: 'Under what circumstances should an advertiser stop using one medium only (meaning TV) and switch to another (meaning magazines)?'

Another question asked concerned the 'problem of frequency'. *Newsweek* asked various research companies for their ideas. The problem was put in these terms: 'How does the effect of exposing advertising vary with repetition?' or, in our language, 'What is the response function?' This proposal was written by Joyce, who was then the Chairman of Axiom Market Research Bureau in New York, owned by JWT, and McDonald in London.

The proposal reminded readers that the Marketing Science Institute in the US had reprinted McDonald's paper and had aroused interest in the technique. Other US work, using a variety of other methods, had reported similar findings. Attempts to repeat the study in 1973 and 1974 received expressions of support but not enough funding. This was to be the most serious attempt so far to do single-source work again.

A detailed specification was put forward, this time including ad exposure from magazines, newspapers and radio as well as television. Over 100,000 pages of questionnaires were to be completed and analysed. The total cost was one million dollars. It was not raised.

2. A British study in 1985[14] mirrored McDonald's, with nine product fields again, 13 weeks and 250 housewives in an existing purchase panel, who also completed viewing diaries. It repeated his switching analysis and found a rather different shape, which was attributed to the fall in average ratings between 1966 and 1984.

The authors claimed that 'taking the effects of retention and attraction into account, we can estimate the effect of any TV pattern over time on brand share'. It concluded that one-plus cover is 'not a useful measure of the effect of a campaign', and that 'two OTS may be required to have an effect'.

The results were used[15] explicitly to 'fit the effective frequency concept into media planning ... to maximise the proportion of a target population receiving say 2 to 3 OTS within a period equivalent to the product's average purchase cycle'. The method was called 'effective reach'.

3. When I was working in Chicago, one of my tasks was to look at the 'academic tapes' which IRI had released from their BehaviorScan data. This admirable gesture had produced some results from the university researchers who tried to unravel the behaviour described. Most of them failed to find advertising effects and claimed that the data only emphasised the power of promotions. The consensus was that advertising effects were too weak to show. This was not good news for advertising agencies, and my job was to find the effects. My previous work with time series of data from separate sources (sales and prices and distribution on one hand, advertising on the other, represented by adstock) made people at Burnett hopeful that it could be adapted to the new data. I was given a team and set to work.

Like the academics, I failed. Eventually my boss, Josh McQueen, called me in. My time was re-allocated to work which was more likely to bear fruit. The team was broken up.

What I did find, and published,[16] was not only that McDonald's analyses could be replicated, but that much more was going on than he had allowed for. There were price effects, which he had not tried to measure. Adstock seemed to have a linear effect on brand choice, but one factor interacted with another. Contingency tables did not seem the right way to look at the data. I recommended that any future attempt used the fact that the data were multivariate, and did not sweep this richness under the carpet.

Contingency tables have only recently been improved, as we see in Chapter 12. The need for multivariate analyses is also better met now, and is also summarised in Chapter 12.

4. The largest attempt in the UK to repeat Joyce and McDonald's experimental panel, before TvSpan (Chapter 12), was in 1985. At that time, Sue Moseley was Research Director for the ITV Company with the franchise in the Midlands, Central Television (she is currently involved in TVSpan for the TV contractor Meridian). Television was a very profitable business at the time, 'a licence to print money', said Lord Thomson, and this company had a substantial marketing budget which it had not needed to spend.

Moseley, like all of us, knew of the attempts to start a single-source panel. Why not use the cash to set up a panel in her region? The Adlab panel[17] ran until 1990. It was available for general analysis – I did some work with her on the number of ad exposures people experienced, before they first decided to try a certain new heavily advertised brand. Although the campaign had been much criticised for its weight, new trialists were still coming in after far larger numbers of OTS than anyone had previously suggested. No support for Krugman here (see the next chapter for an explanation of 'three hits')! Because the panel was not national, and because there was no 'killer application' – one which everyone wanted, like the spreadsheet on early PCs – Adlab did not survive. But we meet it again later.

Conclusions

This chapter has introduced one of the main players in this story, Colin McDonald. It has shown the central part played by single-source data. Later, we again meet Joyce, McDonald and single source. It turns out that the analysis of purchase occasions and of the viewing panel are important parts of the subject's history.

10   Three hits and other effectiveness theories

*Nothing called effective frequency can ever be simply defined as a
pure number of media exposures*[1]

This chapter reviews the years between McDonald's exploration, and the
analyses of a larger US single-source panel, which is described in the next
chapter. On the way there were many other sources, measures and views on
how advertising worked. I base the story on the career of a single researcher.

Naples at Gallup

Gallup and Robinson was a big employer in Princeton, New Jersey, where
Mike Naples was brought up. It was an obvious place for Naples to go to
work in 1960 – he says it just struck him as an interesting way to earn a
living. He had set out to major in mathematics at Rutgers University, instead
he switched to English literature. He then answered a job ad in the local
paper.

Work started with advertising recall research: asking people what they
remember about an advertisement they may have seen yesterday in a
magazine or on television. While *sales* are what the advertiser really wants,
it was believed at the time that if the ad was not remembered in an interview
then it could not have an effect. Naples accepted this convention.

Since that time, advertising recall has become a controversial measure
among researchers. The model is apparently sensible: if an ad strikes you so
much that you can tell an interviewer more about it than about some other
ad, then it 'must' be more effective.

But what has the advertiser actually learned about the process you
originally went through as you glimpsed or scanned the ad? How much of
what you remember about the *ad* attaches itself to the *brand*? Is what you
remember motivating – is it relevant to what you *do* in the store the next
day? Is an interview at all like shopping? Does it follow that the better
recalled ad is also the more persuasive? The answer to all these questions is
that recall does not actually tell us much about behaviour.

In due course, testing advertisements before they went on air won out
over these measurements in the field. Laboratory-type numbers were faster

and cheaper; they were collected before the ad had been made and they allowed diagnostics to be collected (the reasons *why* the ad works as it does).

Naples at Levers

In 1966 Naples had moved to New York, and started his 15 years in the large corporate research department of Levers. Unilever is one of the few companies to invest seriously in market research – and has seen it pay off. There could be no better place to establish a career based on the study of marketing effectiveness.

Here Naples also had the guidance of Bill Moran, to whom he owed his statistical training and much more. He says he traces his way of doing things directly to Moran.

A lot of the learning in Levers came from experiments.[2] It looks fairly easy to run different copy, or to use a different weight of advertising, in various cities or marketing areas. The measure for the sales effect of a campaign was hunted mainly in this way. There are classical experimental designs to follow: 'What you want is a Latin square design', Moran might say.

Naples took it as his mission to show that measuring advertising effects by marketplace testing, of a single variable at a time, was in his words 'appropriate, do-able and rewarding'. But even careful designs do not always lead to clear answers. Despite the trouble Levers took, many experiments had to be written off. More haphazard companies failed even more often. I myself saw a very low success rate when I worked in Chicago and looked at experiments carried out in the Eighties.

One cause was the poor matching of time periods and of area definitions when they came from different sources. You can imagine the fuzziness of the numbers, which were meant to measure quite rapid effects, when sales data were collected only at two-month intervals, and from districts which were not identical to the advertising lay-down.

Another reason was the disturbing effect of competitors' activities – deliberate or not – on the overall result. There were also large and purely random variations in sales, compared with the size of the desired advertising effects. Either of these could be devastating. Too often, they swamped the real results.

Naples saw two points. First, there had to be a better way to learn than from the slow, fumbling and risky process of field testing. It also showed your hand to your competitors. Second, the lessons were too crude in another way: you found out *what* worked, but not *why*. There was not enough information about the individual reaction, about the way in which ad exposures actually caused change.

Applying the strong theory of advertising

Ever since direct effects on sales were abandoned in the 1950s as the classical way to measure and understand the effects of advertising, the industry had been searching for an alternative.

The dominant model at that time in the US was the strong theory which Joyce attacked in the last chapter: seeing an ad was like an instruction. And consumers did as they were told. All the researchers had to do was find out exactly how the instructions were being passed on.

With the data about sales coming from the shoppers' panels, and the data about TV coming from the new viewers' panels, the connection should be easy to find. If the operational researchers had returned from the war with the ability to save pilots' lives, or improve the plans to recover the Pacific islands from the Japanese, surely they could measure the effects of a force as powerful as advertising?

Unfortunately, they could not. The mental model simply did not work in practice. Shoppers, it appeared, could not be told what to do. Soldiers and sailors obeyed orders, most of the time, but consumers were cussed. Whatever the connection was, other forces masked any visible effect. With growing consumer choice (in the US) sales seemed harder to control. Other ways of spending the marketing budget increased. Rather than compete with them through evidence of sales effects, reliance on sales as the measure for advertising fell out of fashion.

The official view was published in 1961, but had been brewing for years before that. 'Advertising is for communication – measure its communication effects'. This was the recommendation of one of the most influential book-lets [3] ever published on advertising, with the title *Defining Advertising Goals for Measured Advertising Results*, known as DAGMAR.

This listed the reasons why sales were *not* the right goal. They were too much affected by a formidable list: price, product, packaging, point of purchase, promotion, personal selling and other publicity. Instead, the new techniques of consumer surveys were to be used to set targets for advertising.

Shoppers were still being treated as sheep, but the gates they were to be driven through were re-named. They began in ignorance. Then they were informed, their attitudes were influenced and their propensity to buy increased; finally, they were converted to the advertised brand. All the surveys had to do was to measure what stage they had reached in this process, and how intense their feelings were. The advertising effect on them was thought to be large or small in the same proportion as whether the score in a survey was high or low.

Apparently the logic could not be faulted; the results were gratifying. Usually, campaigns did what they were now supposed to do. Research scores responded; the budgets rolled in. This is still a powerful philosophy, 40 years later. A speaker from the management consultants, McKinsey, said at a conference[4] in London in 1996: 'In our experience, advertising objectives can rarely be set in terms of sales results; instead they must focus on what advertising can reasonably hope to achieve', which we were later told was awareness, image and stated buying intentions.

New direct measurements

By 1973, Naples felt[5] we were recovering from the misguided retreat of DAGMAR. We were 'in the midst of a period of significant achievement'. He was optimistic on two grounds. First, there were now 'electronic cash registers' – we had the ability to capture accurate and rapid sales data. Second, 'two-way cable TV' – the possibility of knowing whether households had tuned their set to our commercial, and of setting up TV experiments. These developments 'are teasing us with their promise of even more precise advertising research applications'.

Research companies were initially encouraged by such positive forecasts and by the existence of enough companies like Levers who would pay for better understanding. In part, their reaction was justified over the next 20 years. But only in small ways, significant for what was learned and with some commercial failures. In 1994 Naples identified[6] only three applications (in the US), all of which were discontinued. Naples gave cost as the biggest reason, especially the expense of capturing all the schedule data (what commercials were transmitted?) and combining it with viewing by members of the panel (were they tuned to this station?).

The three attempts were:
- *Adtel split-cable Television Testing System* in Charleston, West Virginia, which grew out of an ARF feasibility study and was used throughout the 1970s for testing.
- *BehaviorScan* added meters to a subset of homes in the 1980s; commercial schedules were added to the records manually.
- *Nielsen* added meters to a subset of their Household Panel and Monitor-Plus added the commercial schedules. These data are the subject of the next chapter.

The new subject – data on buying and viewing from the same people – in Naples' view took more time to be accepted, and needed more promotion in the industry, than it should have done. He was correct in expecting that the experience companies gained from the new data was valuable; but it was so valuable that they were unwilling to talk about it. In his Levers' experience, he saw a company leading the industry – sharing much of what it knew in order to push forward the whole.

This is rare in secretive corporate America today. I once tried to get the American Association of Advertisers to support a scheme like the one I started in London, for advertising effectiveness case histories. In New York, they looked at me oddly, 'You mean, publish case histories showing why we are successful? Helping our competitors?'

Finally, the subject got pushed down the agenda by other concerns, particularly promotions.

Fewer experiments

These attempts not only provided improved data, they attempted to replace existing methods of collecting and using marketplace data, especially in experiments. Ironically, the same competitors who, unwittingly or not, had made results hard to read, were now necessary to provide enough work for the research companies to make costs reasonable.

Statistical skills sorted out the interference problem when it was not too severe. For example, suppose it is your brand's price, relative to competitors' prices, which caused most variation in your sales. You cannot always control even your own brand's price, since retailers make so many of your consumer pricing decisions. You certainly cannot manage your competitors' prices. Yet it is precisely price, relative to competitors' prices, which affects sales so much.

Suppose you launch into this marketplace a test of new advertising copy. How can you expect to see the effect if it is concealed by the larger swings in sales due to price? The answer is to measure the price effects too, and then take them into account, but methods[7] to do this are still little used.

Mistaken optimism

In 1968 Leo Burnett bought the agency I then worked for in London. I had, for the first time, direct access to American experience and I began to share Naples' optimism. Where I had previously written, in the first edition of a book[8] about media planning, 'Evaluating a campaign is a short-term operation ... and may indicate in which direction advertising should move ... (but) we should not expect to observe much more than straws in the wind', I felt able to add, in the second edition, five years later, 'Despite these problems, I recommend that, whenever possible, advertising is made accountable'.

A bigger problem Naples observed was the impatience of advertisers. 'Why should we worry about the long term?' They might have added, 'What has posterity ever done for us?' It is likely that the long-term effects of advertising are more important than the short-term effects, and Naples believed such effects were measurable in principle. But this is rarely attempted, for three reasons.

- First, because there was – and still is – no generally accepted technique.
- Second, 'Don't keep a dog and bark yourself'. Advertisers passed the problem to their agencies. They were paid to do the advertising – they should be the experts – they should justify themselves. Sometimes the result of this attitude is that the best people in manufacturing do not gravitate to the study of advertising effectiveness – because they rarely get real responsibility. So the job falls between two stools. There are faster routes for advancement than research in a difficult and controversial area.
- Third, because of the low priority given to the question. The short-term orientation of Western managers discourages it. They are more likely to get notice by claiming, 'Here's a great quick result!' Later on, when it is found they have mortgaged the farm, it may be too late to catch up with them.

A 1978 review

Zielske's work (summarised in Chapters 4 and 5) was included as one of about 150 articles in a review[9] written nearly 20 years later. This begins, as articles about media so often do, by lamenting the good old days when more advertising could be afforded. Ever-increasing costs, and the rising noise level, meant a search for more effective scheduling. Perhaps flighting is the answer. However, sensibly in my view, factors are listed which could swing the decision either way and the overall conclusion is: it depends.

Some 'suggestive evidence' is quoted, which led to a formula which could be applied to a variety of schedules. The conclusions were:

- if your share of voice is high, be continuous;
- if it is low, you can increase the average remembrance level by flighting, as well as reaching higher peaks (however 'flights' then meant very short gaps – one week was recommended; media costs have continued to rise since and longer gaps are now common).

Effective Frequency

Naples' best-known publication[10] *Effective Frequency* was started at about this time, appearing finally in 1979. The subtitle is *The relationship between frequency and advertising effectiveness*. Both the history and the contents of this book are important.

He served on the Research Policy Committee of the Association of National Advertisers. Its members were aware of a rag-bag of studies about an important question. If it could be answered, they would get help in deciding both the best size of an advertising budget and the way the commercials bought on TV should be spread over time. The question may be put: 'Can we say that an ad has to be seen a certain number of times before it works?', or, 'What effects do we get from different levels of ad pressure?'

The phrasing is deliberately vague. The different reports summarised in Naples' book do not use consistent definitions. When he says, 'seen a certain number of times', he does not make clear whether or not the ad has been seen before, or over what period he counts the number of times. 'Before it works' seems to imply it did not work before – but suddenly does; or, there might be some thinking about return on investment here, and he may be looking for pay-offs at various frequencies. What is 'ad pressure' at the moment of purchase, from previous advertising? Some ads are more effective than others, of course, but also some ad exposures occurred longer ago than others.

It is significant that the task Naples undertook in writing *Effective Frequency* was not a popular one. No other member of the committee stepped forward to help. Either they knew too little about the subject, or they thought the effort to summarise what was already known was not worthwhile.

He later reported[11] that he reviewed over 500 public and private sources for the book, but only 50 were summarised, as there were 'surprisingly few well-designed studies that were germane'.

The book's most infamous conclusion is that the first exposure, however defined, is 'simply inadequate'. Achenbaum is quoted as 'best articulating the whole concept'; he goes further and says the first *and* second OTS are ineffective.

In retrospect, I believe the key to what now seems a surprising summary is a difference in mental models. Nowadays, we are usually interested in the average response over the schedule. The response to a single exposure may be, in Naples' words, 'simply too small'. He requires a reaction which is large, even if momentary.

I have some sympathy with this criterion, though I think it is incorrect. In practice, it is hard to say to an advertiser, 'I know you haven't seen any clear reaction to this schedule, but the average is up by a small amount'. Hitting some target level in awareness, for example, may have been a criterion. The Zielske data show this point very clearly. To demonstrate that the advertising is working, it seemed better to concentrate the advertising and then point at the high resulting peak. Even if the area under the slow growth reaction to the continuous schedule is larger, can we be so sure that advertising is the cause? A heavy-up test is sometimes recommended for a similar reason, 'Let's demonstrate a result which is beyond any doubt.'

Priemer suggests another angle: much advertising is simply irrelevant to most shoppers, who are not 'in the market' at the time. Measures of effect taken over a total universe, like awareness, are rarely going to move much at one OTS.

A neglected conclusion was that 'there must be experimentation with each brand to determine its own frequency-of-exposure response function'. This must have seemed quixotic, and is still an ideal. It amazes me that many people expect a single response function or effective frequency for every campaign, when they are ready to accept big differences across brands in ad effectiveness, response to price changes and so on.

The author quoted in the book who appeals to me most is Benesch, who lists factors to be taken into account in discussing the frequency of OTS. Today we would write a different list, but the principle, that the scheduling decision is made after the budget decision and is subject to situation-specific factors, cannot be stressed too much.

A major section in this book was a long summary of McDonald's analysis. At the time, this tiny study was the most-quoted learning for the effect of repeated opportunities to see. Surely this approach could be repeated by those eager for improvements in effectiveness?

One of the most powerful papers in this field[12] was quoted in the book, Herb Krugman's 'three hit theory' for which the strongest support was psychological theory about learning. At the first exposure there is an attempt to understand the nature of the stimulus: 'What is it?' At the second, there is an evaluative response: 'What of it?' Finally, there is 'true reminder – or perhaps the beginning of disengagement'. But, confusingly, the same person might months later 'experience the 23rd exposure as if it were the second'.

This is clearly a think-piece; it is not a report on actual data. However, hard evidence was in short supply, and planners were desperate for guidance of any kind, so Krugman was quoted as evidence for three as *the* effective frequency. Planners simply did not read the paper carefully enough, as Ephron points out in Chapter 12.

McDonald believes[13] that one of the reasons his 1966 results were so acceptable was because they 'appeared to provide some welcome behavioural confirmation of the Krugman hypothesis that two or three exposures are an optimal level'.

It is fairly clear that 'works' meant to Naples, 'increases the chance of a sale', but not all those whose work was reported meant the same. Does it imply some introspection by the shopper, some attitude change? Is the response changing a habit? Creating one? Overcoming a higher price for the brand?

Naples did not solve all these dilemmas, nor did he guide the reader through the hard decisions needed to make the answers precise. But these are comments made with hindsight. It is difficult for us to picture how unformed the subject was at the time. The right follow-up questions were simply not being asked; clarity in defining the main question did not seem necessary – and a direct answer could not be given anyway. What he did was to report the most relevant learning and beliefs from others.

As Naples pointed out, 'we were really only beginning to scratch the surface', and he predicted, optimistically, that further useful long-term marketplace experimentation will take place in the 1980s'. In 1997 he was more sanguine, writing rather harshly that 'the difficulty and expense of obtaining and analysing single source data needed to unlock media strategy information has not resulted in any new learning. ... There is no recent marketplace experience body of knowledge of any worth to guide media planners'.

Looking back, the concept of effective frequency had enjoyed a long history before Naples reported that it had 'gained substantial acceptance among media planners'. This has been amply and independently confirmed.

In 1976, Charles Ramond, then speaking from the Advertising Research Foundation, said:[14] 'Pulsed advertising can generate more sales per dollar than steady advertising', and in support he quoted studies by DuPont and Budweiser. An internal Leo Burnett review at the time recommended pulsing generally, but warned that at high budget levels the planner must bear in mind diminishing returns and possible irritation of the viewer. Also, marketing factors such as seasonality must be taken into account.

In the same year, Bill Moran reported[15] data (based on awareness studies) which supported flighting. For example, three ads per four-week period increased awareness by 31 per cent if spaced, but by 44 per cent if pulsed. The following year he recommended[16] a system of regular awareness studies, plus modelling from such data, to build schedules.

In 1978 a UK survey[17] reported that 87 per cent of managers responsible for advertising decisions believed that threshold effects operated in their markets on levels of expenditure and frequency of exposure. A US review[18] in 1986 concluded, 'in the area of advertising budgets, the practice of pulsing over time and spending beyond threshold levels is well established'. Even in 1994, the overwhelming majority[19] of US agencies judged the effectiveness of their media plans by the three-plus criterion.

Effective Frequency day

Two years later, in 1981, Naples left Levers and was appointed President and CEO of the Advertising Research Foundation. He could now advance the causes in which he believed. One of the methods was to call seminars at which leaders in various fields debated their theories. Two examples follow: one took place the year after his appointment and the other took place 15 years after the publication of *Effective Frequency*.

The ARF held a 'key issues workshop' to discuss effective frequency. Its findings and promises were reviewed four years later, enough time to see whether its promises had been fulfilled. Jack Sissors, a former practitioner turned academic, edited a collection of papers.[20] His verdict was that the 1982 debate was between researchers, not practical people, and 'unfortunately (they) did not help media planners as much as it was hoped they would. Not much progress has been made'. Hence these later papers appeared in a more down-to-earth journal, to give advice to planners on how to use the concept.

The ARF also organised an 'Effective Frequency Research Day' in 1994 at which industry leaders still publicly disagreed with each other, as the following examples show. Worse still, the problems of definition, let alone recommended action, remained unresolved.

The background, as we have seen, is that at this time flighting or pulsing was the norm. The scheduling question was only how big the pulses should be, or equivalently, how many there should be. In order to decide this, some criterion was needed. It was a mechanical problem, not a difference of approach.

At this time, if you asked a buyer what his effective frequency was, you would get a firm answer, but not a very good reason for giving it. The answer was certainly not 'One', because Naples' book had dismissed that. It might be 'Two', as there were still echoes of McDonald's finding. It was likely to be 'Three', from Krugman's 'Three hits' theory. It might be a larger number.

Frequency of what? McDonald[21] called this question a red herring, because the only thing we can measure in real life is an 'opportunity to see'. He also 'set the record straight' and withdrew his s-shaped response as a general rule – as he said it was 'widely misunderstood'.

His reaction to the attention that was paid to effective frequency by media departments is that 'the experimental evidence had never been built up to anything like a sufficient level to carry the huge edifice of effective frequency which came to be placed on it'. He describes this failure as 'a major disappointment', due partly to technical difficulties but more to lack of will and organisation.

Alvin Achenbaum is equally respected, and his 1977 paper 'Effective Exposure' had great influence. He suggested that only three to ten exposures on an individual might count as effective. It was clear he then meant ordinary OTS. Now [22] he said, 'We should only be interested in actual or real exposure, and not exposure opportunities'. His best guess was that only one half of the opportunities were actually taken. Hugh Cannon said the proportion varied between 20 per cent and 85 per cent.

Leo Bogart,[23] another guru, pointed out that the time over which frequency is measured is 'remarkably neglected in the literature on optimum frequency'. In any case, effective frequency was only rarely set as a goal in a sample of media plans, and in this minority there was 'virtually no rationale', said Donald Evanson.[24]

Achenbaum's explanation for this disarray was that the media job had been 'disparaged, reduced and aborted in favour of the so-called creative function'. In other words, agencies spent money on writing ads, but not on placing them, so little had been spent on the problem.

What strikes me about the chaos of this meeting is that the industry leaders, accustomed to laying down the law, seemed to expect a magic, universal number. Workers at the coalface were more realistic. An article[25] a little earlier in a trade magazine, reporting interviews with planners about the repetition of print ads, began its summary with three very down-to-earth points we could all agree with today:
- Do determine your client's goal/objective.
- Do realize that different rules apply to different products.
- Do remember that the nature of both the product and the creative has an impact on frequency.

McDonald's rewritten version

Naples' book[26] was completely rewritten by Colin McDonald in 1996. Again, it seemed impossible to give a final answer to any of the questions. The new version bears too many marks of its original, for example, an effective or optimal OTS level of two or three within a purchase cycle remains a recommendation, though it is now stated with certain reservations. Ephron reviewed the book critically, as we see in the next chapter.

It is nevertheless an important compendium of research reports. It is a good source of his own analysis of the 1976 data, with useful comments from hindsight. There are over 110 references and a section on print. Best of all, McDonald makes it very clear where facts end and speculation begins.

Summing up

A useful perspective on these years appears in two appendices on the history of single-source research in Jones' book.[27] He of course credits McDonald with its first use, but says the method became practical on a large scale only with supermarkets scanning the universal product code.

Media planning use of the sources then took priority, in order to examine the OTS distribution of product-defined targets, so as to determine whether effective frequency had been achieved. This, he believes, drove scheduling towards burst advertising, which is wasteful.

Next, attention moved to the way in which promotions were linked to sales volume. These effects are easily seen and popular with managers – but uneconomic. Thus, the two major uses of the sources have diverted attention from the original idea – to measure the effects of advertising. Individuals have published small pieces of analysis, but never in an easily generalised form and so little used by manufacturers, who 'have progressively lost interest in advertising'. The only exception (before Jones' own work) has been IRI's study of advertising upweight tests, which is a special and increasingly rare case (reviewed in Chapter 4). Finally, he lists the benefits to expect from routine measurement of advertising effects.

Naples has made similar points to me. He says regretfully that he did not foresee that promotion effects would so fascinate managers. Scanner data pushed advertising to the back seat, because response to deals and price cuts was so obvious. The temptation is to compare the two – advertising and promotions – directly on their short-term returns. The result has been the growth of promotions in the US marketing budget at the expense of advertising. No matter that so many promotions are not really expenditure but loss of revenue, no matter that longer-term effects of advertising are not credited – the short-term return has 'been measured' and advertising has been the loser.

11   Once (recently) is enough

This chapter is again about pioneers. It is also about the foundations of the modern vogue for continuous scheduling.

John Philip Jones and 'Once is enough'

In 1953 a 21-year-old Welshman joined the research subsidiary of J.Walter Thompson. After some research experience, John Philip Jones set his sights on a job in the advertising agency. In 1957, he moved to the London office of J.Walter Thompson. There was no better place in Europe to learn the business. It was then known as 'the university of advertising' and for several good reasons. It had wide connections with the New York office and had strong international clients. Jones worked with major companies like Unilever, Beecham, Gillette, Nestlé, Pan American, Pepsi-Cola, Quaker Oats and Scott Paper. JWT and its research subsidiary also had an exceptional ideas group, as we saw in Chapter 9, including Timothy Joyce, Stephen King, Colin McDonald and Tom Corlett.

Later, he worked on the Continent, in Amsterdam and Copenhagen, becoming head of client services in Scandinavia. He found that he taught easily; with his experience of several countries and product categories, he was a natural part of the JWT training programme.

He then made a move for which I know no parallel. He not only left the commercial world, he crossed the Atlantic to become a professor. The stories he could tell from his JWT days furnished his students with raw material which was more practical than most. He stayed up to date, travelled and consulted. From 1986 the books and articles started to pour from his study. In 1991 the American Advertising Federation named him Advertising Educator of the Year.

His view of data analysis matches the habits of both teacher and account director. Since the conclusions have to be easily communicated to learners, and to non-technical members of a brand team, they must always be simply expressed. He believes that our reaction to an explanation should be, 'Of course!' A question we come to later is whether all situations can be so reduced, but there is no doubt about the ease with which simple ideas can be made to affect decisions, compared with complicated ones.

Nielsen single source in the US

In 1987 The NPD Group and the A.C.Nielsen Company started a joint venture in the US. Steve Coffey was seconded from The NPD Group – to which he later returned. He is a market researcher who has specialised in data collection technology. After Columbia, he learned the basic skills at Pillsbury. His job was to create purchasing panels, using the new in-home scanning techniques. The sample had to be designed, recruited and maintained, the in-home equipment installed and made to work, and the data had to be organised.

You are familiar with the bar code on every grocery item you buy – which the clerk at the checkout counter passes over a scanner. This code tells the store computer the brand, the size of the pack and the store price. In a modern shopping panel, a hand-held scanner is given to the participant to keep at home. As the bags are unpacked, the scanner is passed over the purchases. This time the data do not go to the store till, but to the research company.

Nielsen Household Services (separate from their retailer work) developed a number of panels. Three concern us here. The largest was a national panel of 15,000 households, to which 25,000 households were added in local market panels. To some of these households, two other services were attached. One was about reading, the other about viewing.

Joyce reappears

Steve Coffey is proud that he was able to recruit Joyce as a consultant for the collection of readership data from all 40,000 households. This massive enterprise, called HomeScan, had to be designed, analysed and sold. Joyce's background in print and product research, with his reputation for innovation and sound data collection, made him an admirable acquisition by Nielsen. After various profitable enterprises in press research, Joyce could afford to work only where he found it interesting to do so. He was therefore fortunately available at a critical stage. Coffey described him to me as 'the brains behind HomeScan'.

The main purpose of Joyce's work was to create a service that described readership in terms more meaningful than demographics. It was possible, says Coffey, to tell Unilever – and *Women's Day Magazine* – that the readers of that title accounted for, say, $35 million sales a year of Tide laundry detergent.

Its aim was to offer audience data for newspapers and for up to 150 magazines, with purchasing information about the readers in addition to demographics. The scanning method was adapted for this purpose.

In addition, for up to 5,000 households in the national panel, TV set or household meters were added. It was debated at the time whether the additional information provided by people meters was worth the additional trouble – both to the household and in analysis. This is still a difficult decision, since personal exposure to TV and personal purchase decisions are the stuff of true single-source data. In fact the roles of the shopper and of individual consumers in a household are complex, which is one reason we cannot expect clean results.

This panel was known as the single-source database; its analysis is our main subject in this chapter. It ran only from 1991 to 1993. The accuracy of the meter data can be questioned. It has been said, for example, that households with large disposable incomes, Hispanics and dwellers in high rises are under-represented.[1] But whatever their weaknesses, they were the best single-source data then available and they were certainly good enough for the work which follows.

When these vast panels were up and running, Nielsen felt confident enough to buy The NPD Group's interest in the joint venture; the projects then became a division of Nielsen.

Thus, in the early 1990s there were two Nielsen single-source panels: HomeScan, with purchasing and reading data, and the purchasing and viewing panel.

Joyce has told me that his private forecast was that the TV panel was not going to get anywhere. He had seen the failure to arouse American interest in re-creating the panel he had piloted in London. It was not clear what analyses to do on the TV panel, nor who was to be its guiding light. However, he gave what assistance he could and Nielsen hoped to home-grow the answer. He introduced Jones to Nielsen, as we see later. He discussed with Jones his analyses, and he gave some warnings, but it was not his work. He was more interested in the related venture to set up MonitorPlus, the system that recorded what commercials were on air. This used pattern recognition, a technique in which he took a keen interest, and later planned to use in information retrieval.

The databases were now only just controllable with the computing power available. Even Nielsen, who had already mastered the bar-code system which identified products and pack sizes, and ran a TV ratings service, found that putting the two together strained their resources. It was a serious task to support and continuously update the systems, code files and household records. In addition, Nielsen had to compete – often on price – with other suppliers of similar products – notably IRI and Arbitron.

In Jones' book, described later, there is an admirable description of the Nielsen source and the files that Jones extracted. Briefly, 2,000 households were used. At the till, the store computer could work out what the price was, whether this was a multibuy and so on. At home, where the pack might have come from any store, the bar codes could not be used for this; the shopper had to enter the price and any promotions noted.

The meters attached to the TV sets in these households recorded the stations tuned to (but not who was in the room). Viewing was matched with logs kept by MonitorPlus of the advertisements transmitted. In this way, the system collected details of the household's opportunities to see brand advertising, though not necessarily by the shopper who recorded purchases.

Two uses of the data

Obviously Nielsen was anxious to find links between advertising exposure and sales behaviour. Without them, a major part of their investment had no market.

The first application is before a campaign: are there better ways to describe the target audience, on which planning decisions are based, than by the demographics in normal industry panels? In a phrase, to provide 'buyer ratings'. It is by sales of Tide (or other brands) – or rather by the households where these decisions are made – that viewing is described. By 1991 such analyses were possible. The results were impressive efficiency gains in TV planning, according to George Shababb, Director of Operations for Nielsen Household Services.

The aim was to improve the schedule and its allocation,[2] that is 'the constant juggling of cost management, corporate ownership, brand goals, make-goods, programme changes and copy availability'. Case histories were published showing in some cases real improvements in efficiency.

There were too few purchasers for this service. It meant moving outside the safe perimeter of current practice. In addition, it assumed that historic buyer ratings for a TV series, channel or daypart would provide, in the future, better guidance than the demographics. Planners accepted this argument for magazines; they understood how these attracted particular audiences consistently. They found it less convincing for television, with its greater volatility.

The second use of the panel, and the one of interest in this book, is like McDonald's in Chapter 9: where the panel is used after a campaign, to describe its effect on sales. Coffey describes the resources put to this work as 'substantial'. That was just within Nielsen Household Services. The parent, Nielsen Marketing Research, with its great experience, statistical skills and computing resources, was also brought in.

Why did Nielsen, and IRI faced with a similar problem, fail to capitalise fully on their single-source panels? Why did my approach, when I was working at Leo Burnett, Chicago, not work either? Why were most academics, working with the IRI tapes, unable to find advertising effects? There are three reasons. First, the computing power available in those days now looks too limited. What might now take seconds then took overnight runs. Second, the models behind the computing were just too complicated. Nielsen brought in the chaos of the supermarket and all the pressures there on the shopper. I allowed for all the variety of individual households. Each of us added the dimensions we knew best. Nielsen was used to the store environment; with an agency background, I was used to thinking of individuals and single campaigns. Third, the way the advertising parts of the models were formulated did not correspond closely enough to the real world. The data remained inscrutable.

The failure to get usable results about advertising from the single-source panel took place at some remove from Joyce's more successful work with the readership panel. Yet it intrigued him. Surely the data were the same as he had collected and McDonald had analysed all those years ago? The single source was alive – why was it not yielding?

Jones meets the data

It was a happy coincidence that Joyce had also moved from England to the US, and that the two expatriates saw each other from time to time. Jones was always on the lookout for numbers he could use. Joyce had helped him before with data from another source he controlled – Mediamark – which started in 1979 and which Jones had analysed for an earlier book.

Joyce introduced him to the right people. By 1992 he had signed a contract for a new book and was at work. At the end of 1992 he was circulating some results privately – in December, he was corresponding with me and with others about his ideas.

He was not the only outside analyst working with the panel. Advertisers had access: some of them had passed data on to Walter Reichel, who appears later in this chapter.

Why did Nielsen give Jones access to the data – and more than that, practical help in analysing it his way? We have seen that the company was desperate for findings that would justify its investment, and demonstrate the elusive link between ad exposure and choice of the brand. The situation calls to mind mineral prospecting. The company has paid millions for the rights. It is sure the gold or the oil is there, but no one can find it. Then out of the blue appears the lone prospector, the confident and experienced explorer, with a record of finds.

Coffey now remembers Jones as the first academic to lay out a scheme which Nielsen found convincing. His confidence was unquestionable. His credentials in publication were impeccable – and Nielsen needed the publicity. Joyce had inspired McDonald's earlier work. Joyce and Jones suggested that the earlier idea of a universe of purchase occasions made the analyses manageable.

Nielsen tried to drive a bargain. Jones was getting free access to very valuable data. He was the one who would benefit from a book, and whose reputation would grow if he cracked the problem. He should pay at least for the computer time needed. In negotiation, Jones pointed out that a publisher's advance hardly paid for travel expenses between his university at Syracuse and Port Washington, Long Island, where the data were held. What were a few thousands, after so many millions of dollars had already been sunk? Nielsen sensibly agreed.

Now Shababb and Jones got to work together. Shababb had spent a of lot of his own time in the pursuit of effect measures. He knew the data, he was used to trying to tease out its meaning. They started to think about the individual shopping occasion as the basic building block, as McDonald had done and as Reichel had repeated on IRI data. They picked a product group – laundry detergents – and Jones specified the analyses he needed. As these began to show results, more resources were allocated. Eventually three Nielsen analysts were working with Jones.

When ads work

Jones published his book[3] in 1995. Earlier articles had whetted the industry's appetite. He makes claims which fall into three groups.

– First is his measure of short-term sales-effectiveness, which he calls STAS (Short-Term Advertising Strength) and which I explain below. In the analysis of single-source data it is possible[4] 'to isolate one variable while all the others remain constant'. It was the intention, 'which was, I believe, substantially realised, that in its isolation of a single variable, the research would resemble a controlled experiment'.[5]
– Second, he can measure the response to advertising, when sample sizes allow, from any particular number of exposures (one, two and so on). In this analysis[6] he finds that a single exposure increases sales by 11 per cent, while from *any* number of exposures[7] the increase is 14 per cent. Hence 'a single exposure in the seven days before purchase has far greater effect than what is added by further exposures'. It is 'all you need to generate an immediate effect ... diminishing returns set in from the first exposure'. This leads to the recommendation that campaigns should be continuous and 'an advertiser only needs to buy enough ratings to ensure that most viewers in his target group will see one of his advertisements (in a week)' – hence the summary, 'once is enough'.

– Third, 'an advertising campaign must produce a short-term effect before it can generate a long-term one'.

The qualities which all these claims have in common are simplicity and confidence. This makes them very attractive to busy and non-technical executives. Like much popular management advice, they are easy to understand and to apply. These are admirable qualities – provided they adequately summarise the evidence.

You will understand that the problem on which this book concentrates now has a claimed solution – a scheduling ideal is laid down. Additionally, the sales effectiveness of the campaign (both short and long term) can be measured.

Undoubtedly, these are the best-known and most influential conclusions drawn from single-source analyses to date. Hence, I go into some detail about them below. As I have pointed out, Jones' instinct is to move things along. Research is important, not just for its own sake, but to be applied. Too many researchers, he believes, concentrate on a small piece of the jigsaw, and never step back to see the picture.

In 1997, Jones modified[8] his claim that flighting and effective frequencies other than one should never be used. He said this was permissible 'in the most exceptional circumstances'. The examples given were new brands and new campaigns (where there 'must still be a Krugman-esque build-up of exposures to get the message across'), highly seasonal goods and services, and the building up of a subscriber base, as for a publication. Details of how the new schedules should be written were not given, but the implication is that three-plus effective frequency is to be used as before.

The actual analyses

Let us go through the steps taken to construct Jones' measure, starting from the data from a single-source panel in the following form, for each shopper in the panel:

– for a selected brand and category (consisting of the brand and its competitors), you know when any one of these brands was bought, and which one,
– for the TV commercials for these brands, you know when the shopper saw one, and
– for which brand.

You can imagine four columns of raw data about a single shopper. There is one row for each day. In the first column we enter a '1' on each day our brand was bought, or leave it blank. In the second column, the same for competitors in total. In the third column we put the number of our ads the shopper saw and in the last column the same for competitors' ads. We have similar sets of columns for every other shopper too.

Note how much simpler this is than the table Joyce published in 1967 (referred to in Chapter 9). The main reduction so far is to 'my brand' and 'all competitors'; more is going to be cut away.

Now ask the question, is there a link between the times our brand was chosen, and the commercials the shopper recently saw? When Jones, and Reichel as we see later, asked themselves this question, they answered it in similar ways. The key was McDonald's idea of analysing 'purchasing occasions'. They used the first and second columns to identify when any brand was bought. This is a purchase occasion.

They made two new columns, where each row now stands for a purchase occasion, not for a day. In the first column, '1' means that our brand was chosen, while a blank means that some competitor was picked.

Then, for this occasion, they looked back to the first table to see whether our commercials were seen by this shopper. Jones looked back seven days, Reichel tried this and other time intervals. McDonald, remember, has worked with four days. In the second new column '1' means that at least one of our ads was seen (an 'exposed' occasion), while a blank means that none of our ads was seen.

When they had finished with the construction of these two columns for one shopper, they started on the next one and carried on. At the end they have two columns only, to summarise the information from the whole panel. It has as many rows as the number of times any brand in the category was bought.

If there is '1' in the second column for the same day, this means that the shopper saw at least one of our ads in the chosen time interval before the occasion. There are clearly four possibilities for the pair of cells across the two columns. Hence, all the occasions can be summarised into a single two-by-two table.

We have given up a lot of information in order to get to this point. We have lost the identity of the individual shoppers. Price and promotions do not appear. We have ignored competitors' advertising. For our own advertising, we know only whether or not there was any exposure in the selected interval (though we could have counted the number of OTS, and will in fact do so in another table). We now know nothing about ad exposures longer ago than seven days.

A sample of purchase occasions

In Chapter 6 the OTS distribution was derived from a viewing panel. The process above also gives a set of OTS. Are the two the same?

In so far as heavy viewers have more OTS than light viewers, they are the same. But the viewing panel was a sample of people without regard to their shopping habits. The shopping panel, in contrast, holds only people who shop in the category concerned – it is a sub-sample of all people. And it is a sample of purchase occasions: a heavy purchaser in the category provides more occasions than a light buyer.

So *no* analysis of purchase occasions – McDonald's in Chapter 9, Jones or Reichel in this chapter, Roberts later and my adstock analyses earlier – is comparable with the usual OTS distributions from a viewing panel. The two samples differ in a vital way.

The analyses were reported by Jones over all the occasions in the category. McDonald has done similar work[9] which separated occasions by the different weights of purchase in the category. He concludes, in one example, that for OTS in the purchase interval, light-weight and medium-weight buyers respond to increases in OTS while heavy buyers do not.

How much recent advertising?

Naples has pointed out that Jones is actually not describing the effect of a single, or of a first OTS, but that of the most recent, possibly of a long sequence. When I was debating with Jones in Hong Kong, a city of legendary gamblers, I made use of this fact. Suppose, I argued, we are in a supermarket aisle when a shopper approaches the category fixture. Our job is to forecast which brand will be bought. We are allowed to ask any questions (except 'What will you buy?') and then bet whether or not the shopper will buy our brand.

Jones asks one question only, 'How many of our ads have you seen in the last week?' McDonald, 'What brand did you buy last time? How many of our ads have you seen since then?' In my own single-source analyses, I ask, 'Tell us about all the ads you have seen – exactly when, and whether for us or for a competitor. Also, tell me what share of your total purchases are for our brand. Finally, what price offers or deals are there on the fixture?' I invited the audience to say which method would lead to more correct guesses about which brand was going to be bought. The answer is not difficult: the more we know, the better our understanding and our forecasts.

Let me make explicit the point here about recent advertising history. I feel that to count the number of our OTS in an interval like seven days (or, worse, to note only whether there were 'any' OTS for our brand during that interval) is throwing away too much information. The longer the interval, the more likely it is that the most recent OTS was longer ago; but also the more likely there was more than one OTS. We are bound to get a more confused picture than if we use adstock, which allows precisely for all the previous ads seen. In fact, I have always had a better fit when modelling with adstock than by seeing whether there were any ads in the last few days (which I have also tried).

The STAS calculation

By reducing the data in this way, Jones has bought a very attractive possibility, which completes the work he does at this stage. He can look at the association between seeing one of our advertisements in the week before purchase and choosing to buy our brand. He uses a measure or index[10] known as the 'odds ratio' or 'ratio of percentages'. This is used, for example, in medical research, to study various possible causes for a disease.

He works out our brand shares, or the odds of buying our brand, on the 'unexposed' occasions and on the 'exposed' occasions. He finds their ratio, dividing the second share by the first (and multiplying the result by 100).

An imaginary example will make this clear. Suppose there are only six purchase occasions, and they fall as follows:

	Not exposed to advertising	*Exposed to advertising*	*Total*
Bought the brand	1	2	3
Didn't buy the brand	2	1	3
Total	3	3	6
Brand share	1/3	2/3	3/6

Now divide the second share (two-thirds) by the first (one-third) to get the odds ratio (here 2), and multiply the result by 100 to make the index (here 200). This means that the brand share is twice as high on the exposed occasions.

Here 2/3 are the 'odds' for buying (catching the illness) for those exposed to advertising (with the treatment studied). The correct test of significance for this ratio compares two binomial distributions, but in our applications the numbers of occasions are usually large and this is not necessary.

Jones claimed that practical consequences should follow from the measure: 'Change the campaign, if STAS is low.'

The STAS average for his 78 brands is 124. For 22 of the brands the index was below 100. (The proportion of choices of our brand was lower in the exposed group, the average for which was 84.) For the rest the average was 139.

If the table above had come from an experiment and if the only difference between the exposed and unexposed occasions was in fact seeing the ads, the index and the advice above would be very convincing. But *is* the process just described 'like an experiment'? Are the 'exposed' and 'unexposed' occasions similar in every way – except that some of them happened to have advertising shortly before?

These are questions which several analysts have asked. We cannot answer them about Jones' data, since these are no longer available. We have first to specify what sort of complications we have in mind, and then find our own data to check whether they exist. It turns out that there are two possibilities particularly worth looking out for. The most obvious is when advertising is timed with, or actually supports, a promotion. This is good marketing, as there is usually synergy between the two. But good marketing makes for difficult analysis, and in such a case a promotion effect may wrongly be read as an advertising benefit. This is covered in the next chapter.

The second is that, in certain conditions, losing the information about the various individuals who make up the panel could be serious.

Purchase/Viewing bias

How can the fact that we have lost information about individuals make a difference? It is because two particular measures about individuals are likely to be associated. The measures are their normal brand choice and their weight of viewing.

If these are connected, we call this Purchase/Viewing association. This may be positive – people with high loyalty to the brand are also heavy viewers. It may be negative – people with high loyalty to the brand are light viewers.

Overall, there is little association between weight of viewing and the total amount of shopping. For this, the following table[11] shows the flat relationship between the first and second columns, despite the extreme effect on total viewing in the third column:

Quintile by weight of viewing	Percentage of purchases	Percentage of viewing
Light	19	7
2	21	12
3	20	18
4	21	24
Heavy	19	39

The definition of Purchase/Viewing association is not about all purchasing – or even buying in the category as a whole. It is about choosing a specific brand within the category. What is the proportion of my brand's buyers (among all category buyers) among the heavy third of TV viewers, compared with its share among the light third? The ratio of these odds is the definition of the index we use to measure the association.

Here is an example. Take Bird's Mild Coffee, and compare this with Nestlé's Gold Blend, a rather bitter 'coffee-lovers' brand. Because of the demographics of buyers of these brands – and of television viewers – it happens that the Purchase/Viewing index for Mild coffee is above one, or *positive*. People who prefer the blander blend are older, downgrade and watch more commercial television than average. But the index for Gold Blend is below one (*negative*). That is, people who prefer the bitter coffee are younger, more upgrade and watch less commercial TV.

More about Purchase/Viewing bias and STAS

The example above was anecdotal. Two more serious analyses are now given.

The first uses survey data[12] from the US. There were 364 brands in 11 of the 12 categories which Jones analysed. The informants were 'primary users' of each brand. From their viewing claims they were divided into light, medium and heavy viewers.

To create the Purchase/Viewing index I divide the brand's share of category purchase claims among heavy viewers by the share among light viewers. This odds ratio is multiplied by 100. As with STAS, the average for this measure over all the brands was positive (it was 113). For the majority of brands it was over 100. For 22 per cent of the brands it was below 90, for 37 per cent it was over 110; so, for the majority, the bias was over 10 per cent.

The second example[13] shows an association between the index and STAS. I have been working with McDonald on the analysis of UK Adlab and other data. We have found some revealing regularities.

There was even more variation here in the Purchase/Viewing index, as the first row of results shows (remember these are electronically measured data, not claims).

Purchase/Viewing index	Less than 90	Between 90 and 110	Over 110
Number of cases	17	10	25
STAS	97	102	119

The association between the index and STAS is made clearer by dividing the 52 cases at the median by each measure. This leaves little room for doubt that STAS for this data set *is* related to the Purchase/Viewing index (the odds ratio here is 3.3).

	P/V below median	P/V above median	Total
STAS above median	6	20	26
STAS below median	20	6	26
Total	26	26	52

More brands have a positive Purchase/Viewing association than a negative one. How much this is causative is a point for discussion. Did seeing more advertising make them more likely to buy the brands? Perhaps, but there are other factors in the argument, which is not pursued here.[14] All we need to know is whether or not there is a *general* association for a particular brand, not dependent on the accidents of viewing shortly before a purchase in the category.

The conclusion is that we should check our single-source data for possible Purchase/Viewing bias, which Jones did not do. Without this, it is possible that what we see in a high STAS is the sum of two effects, both in the same direction.

If there is a negative Purchase/Viewing bias, it is possible that what we see in a low STAS is the sum of a negative effect – from the bias – and a positive but smaller effect – from advertising. To me, this is more likely than that the occasions when our ad was seen resulted in lower sales (it is suggested, because of competitive effects – if so, why are not competitive effects generally allowed for?). I do not advise changing the campaign solely because STAS is low.

Why does Purchase/Viewing bias affect STAS?

We have just seen associations between the index and STAS – which should be a convincing enough argument to show that this is causative. That is, if a heavy viewer does have a different probability of buying the brand from a light viewer, then will we get STAS different from 100 even if there were no actual effect of advertising?

Consider an imaginary example: heavy viewers who see twice as much TV as light viewers. Then suppose the heavy viewers have an equal chance of buying our brand or not. But the light buyers choose it for only one quarter of their purchases. This example is of a positive Purchase/Viewing bias, since the heavier viewers have twice the proportion of their purchases given to our brand.

Now suppose that we observe 100 buying occasions in each group. For the heavy viewers, just 50 of the purchases will be our brand. For the light viewers, 25 of the purchases will be ours. Suppose further that our advertising schedule is such that the light viewers have been 'exposed' to our advertising 40 times in total on their purchase occasions. The heavy viewers are exposed 80 times.

This is enough information for us to fill in the marginal totals for the same sorts of table as we constructed above.

I have also filled in the cells of the tables, using the null hypothesis that whether the shopper is exposed or not has *no* effect on whether our brand is chosen. That is, our brand's share is exactly the same, within each of these tables, whether the shopper is 'exposed' or not. For the light viewer the share is one quarter in each of the three columns: not exposed, exposed and in total. For the heavy viewer, each share is one half.

Light viewers	*Not exposed*	*Exposed*	*Total*
Bought the brand	15	10	25
Didn't buy the brand	45	30	75
Total	60	40	100
Heavy viewers			
Bought the brand	10	40	50
Didn't buy the brand	10	40	50
Total	20	80	100

It follows that STAS is 100 in each of these tables: share among the exposed is neither higher nor lower than among the unexposed. This was our null hypothesis and there are no surprises so far.

Now let us look at all 200 occasions. That is, we make a new contingency table for all the shoppers, which we get by adding up the cells of these two tables.

All Viewers	*Not exposed*	*Exposed*	*Total*
Bought the brand	25	50	75
Didn't buy the brand	55	70	125
Total	80	120	200

What is the brand share among the exposed in this table? It is 50/120, or as a percentage 42.5. And what is it among the not exposed? It is 25/80 or as a percentage 31.25. We get STAS by dividing 42.5 by 31.25 and multiplying by 100. The result is 136.

At first, you will think I must have got the arithmetic wrong. How is it possible that each of the first two tables shows *no* advertising effect, yet when I add them, I appear to find an effect? I have carefully worked on the assumption that there *is* no effect, yet here is STAS well over 100.

This example has shown that a positive bias meant STAS will be above 100; a similar example with negative bias is easy to write and shows STAS below 100 – *even if advertising has no effect on brand choice at all.* You may make up your own examples and you will find this is always so.

Of course we cannot do this sort of work if we have lost the information about the various individuals who make up the panel. It cannot be done from a single two-by-two summary alone. In real life, I have used tables with finer divisions, to investigate how much of the STAS comes from the Purchase/Viewing bias for the brand, and how much (usually a small proportion) may be really an advertising effect.

Conclusions on STAS

I have now explained two concerns about STAS: the possibilities of confounding with other factors which affect sales, and of Purchase/Viewing bias. They make me worry whether the interpretation of high or low STAS in individual cases is soundly based. I have also mentioned the difficulty of applying purchase occasion findings (which over-emphasise heavy buyers in the category) to industry TV panels (in which each individual features once only).

It is feasible that the extraneous additions to the estimates of ad effects made by STAS are the reason they are so big. Jones reports an average increase of brand share (from unexposed to exposed occasions) of 24 per cent (or, on p 44, 14 per cent). If such large effects of seeing any advertising in the last seven days were normal, it is likely to have been noticed long ago, and to have been frequently confirmed, which is not the case. Remember that McDonald found (for switches, for advertising seen up to four days before) only 1.4 per cent.

An alternative hypothesis is that there is indeed an average short-term effect of advertising, but one which is very much smaller than Jones reported. Purchase/Viewing bias is generally positive, and so usually are other confounding factors, and it could be these which have caused the large average STAS. This is only a hypothesis, but it is the one I prefer and one I have seen confirmed in my own data.

Do the same comments made above about STAS apply to the McDonald and Reichel constructs? Indeed they do. I can show for example that, for brands where the Purchase/Viewing bias is above 100, so as a result are McDonald's statistics for Change and Repeat, even when there is no advertising effect.

Diminishing returns?

Now we look at the report Jones made on the average 'response function'. Here again are his findings for three OTS groups:

OTS	0	1	Any OTS
Brand share, 100 = average at 0 OTS	100	111	114

This simple table is one of the two arguments put forward for scheduling continuously, since it appears that more than one OTS in a week gives little additional benefit; the other is Ephron's 'recency', which is discussed below.

Note that the second group, for one OTS, is included in the third[15] for 'any' OTS. We cannot separate them now. The table with the same headings constructed in Chapter 9 showed that this presentation is not ideal for representing the 'response function'. In that case, the 'Any' group concealed a doubling of the sales effect at two OTS.

In the same year (1995) as Jones published his American book, three pamphlets[16] were published in Germany by the Gesellschaft Werbeagenturen Service (GWA – the association of advertising agencies). In the section most relevant to this story, Jones reported his analysis of 28 German brands in 1993 and 35 in 1994.

Here, the 'response function' was also investigated, though only for brands with positive STAS. Jones gave these results:

OTS	0	1	2	3	4+
1993	100	111	112	117	124
1994	100	107	114	114	129

Here the apparent effect is still climbing after three OTS, and it does not look as though 'once is enough'.

The long term

From Chapter 4 we know one reason why long-term effects matter – they are often needed to show that advertising is economic. This is common ground between most analysts, though a few have denied that advertising can have any effect beyond a few days or weeks. The language used differs, but the majority would agree with Jones:[17]

> *The greatest single influence on a brand's sales is the base equity of the brand. This is a compound of consumers' satisfaction with the brand's functional performance and the added values or psychological rewards*

that come from repeated use of the brand and the advertising campaign working as mutual reinforcements.

He has quoted with approval an analysis where 'brand equity' was credited with 79 per cent of a particular brand's sales, while the short-term effect of advertising was scored at 6 per cent.

There are two other reasons. If long-term effects exist and are not adequately predicted by short-term effects, we may be misled by short-term analyses. Also, Chapter 7 showed that taking them into account in scheduling may alter our plans.

Jones' own test for a long-term advertising effect is whether the brand's sales share grew during the year, a definition I have not seen used elsewhere. For his data, the proportion of 'successes' is almost the same (53 per cent) for non-advertised and advertised brands. I draw the conclusion that the measure cannot be interpreted as an advertising effect. Brands grow and decline in volume sales mainly for other reasons: changes in the product, in distribution, and above all, in price, promotions and competitors' launches, deaths and other activities. Writing about one group of brands in his book,[18] Jones agrees: 'even in these cases, the long-term effect was ... caused by factors other than advertising.' He says elsewhere, 'advertising can even work if sales are going down.'

Jones has also claimed that a short-term effect (his positive or high STAS) is necessary in order for there to be a long-term effect. If so, STAS is a 'gatekeeper' for two reasons. Not only does it tell us whether the campaign has short-term sales effects, it 'represents a screen through which a campaign has to pass before it is capable of generating a long-term effect'.[19]

Thanks to the data given in his book[20] about all 78 advertised brands we can construct this table:

	No 'long-term effect'	'Long-term effect'	Total
High STAS	25	31	56
Low STAS	12	10	22
Total	37	41	78

The key cell here is for low STAS with a 'long-term effect', which is *not* empty. You can compare the observed 10 cases with the expected 11.6 on the null hypothesis that there is no connection (from 22 x 41/78). These two numbers are not so different. I interpret this table as 'no proven association', which is no real surprise, given the nature of the two definitions.

Were all these difficulties discussed at the time?

One of the puzzles in this story is whether, while they were both working at Nielsen, Joyce put to Jones the difficulties I have described. When I asked Joyce about this in 1997, he confirmed that they were ever-present worries to him.

He reminded me that one of his competitors, Starch, had previously come up with a scheme not unlike STAS. This was 'Net Ad Produced Purchases' and was an appealing plan to measure the effect of print advertising[21] – and to justify the noting scores which Starch was selling. Like the Advertising Planning Index in London, this was based on the premise that advertising causes attitude changes which in turn cause purchases. The 'attitudes' in this case were the claims to have noted and the ability to recall press advertising. There were survey data on the scores, and also on intentions to buy or claimed purchasing. Hence, tables could demonstrate whether or not the scores were associated with intentions and claims. Common sense, and the model of advertising many people believed in, were able to interpret causally any connection seen: 'High noting leads to more purchases.'

This fell out of favour, as people realised the flaw which had also been discovered in the UK – purchase change can lead to attitude change, and shoppers are actually more likely to notice and read ads for brands they have just bought. The two questions they are likely to ask themselves are: 'Is there anything about my purchase I ought to know about?' and 'Now is my chance to see whether they are making claims which aren't true'. Plus, of course, the same sort of people may happen to buy the brand and also take more interest in advertising. Or, some people are just more likely to answer 'Yes' in surveys.

All this was reasonably well known in America, and of course very well known to Joyce. How was it then, that the possibility of similar biases was not raised as an objection by Nielsen, or by Joyce? Why were McDonald's switching analyses not repeated? – Joyce had tried hard enough beforehand to encourage this.

Joyce's answer to these questions is remarkable – and as the man on the spot he could make a judgment.

There are very few nuts-and-bolts people – those who have the determination to get a new analysis done – those who are sufficiently expert and trusted to carry the work through, publish it and convince others of their ideas. I can number on one hand the real innovators I have met. Others rely on these experts. They need the leadership, to be told what to do. It is easier for everyone else to go with the flow, to use the currency everyone else is using.

Jones is clearly one of these determined people. And Joyce, as an innovator himself, also had an ability to move on. Immersed for a time in one problem, others soon intrigued him. 'I have no interest in single source now,' he told me in 1997, 'and if I never heard of it again I'd be quite happy.' He probably felt much the same in 1992. Flaws in other people's work do not hold him up. 'If Jones' work is not perfect,' he told me, 'it still ends up in the right place: convex response and more continuous advertising are good advice. I pointed out to him the dangers of missing links.' But it did not much concern Joyce that the warnings were ignored.

Because of Jones' breakthrough, we now know far more about the analysis of single-source data. He changed the tone of the discussion. In Naples' words, 'he opened the industry's eyes to the analysis potential of single-source data.'

More contingency table analyses

Walter Reichel and Leslie Wood have been working with the same data as Jones, and with data from ScanAmerica and IRI. They are commercial analysts, whose firm is A-to-S Link. Their clients are advertisers who could get from Nielsen the data on their own categories.

Nielsen was attracted by the concept. Rather than an historical picture of who or how many buyers bought the brand, their analysis offered for the first time a better understanding of the causality factors.

Some results were published[22] before Jones started work, including the finding that 'a single exposure in close proximity to a purchase occasion exerts a powerful influence on sales'. Note 'proximity'. Like Ephron later, he also emphasised 'propinquity'. McDonald wrote to Reichel in January 1992 about an early publication:

> *I am delighted by the line you take. Yours is the first paper I have seen in twenty years which has actually understood the opportunities opened up by single source research. I fully agree with you about the benefits of disaggregation, the importance of timing factors and the expectation that the answers will vary for different brands, products and advertising (of course – who ever expected advertising to always have the same effect?).*

The ADIMPACT score is slightly different from STAS, though an equally valid way of measuring the same concept. It also starts with the 'buy' share in the exposed group, but divides by the share in the total,[23] not in the unexposed group. In the table above (p.146), 2/3 is to be divided by 3/6, with the result 1.33. This is multiplied by 100 to give 133 and then 100 is subtracted. The index in this case is 33. As already stated, the indices are also worked out over different lengths of time before purchase, from one day through four weeks (commonly used) or up to 12 weeks.

Both STAS and ADIMPACT claim to show how strong our campaign has been in creating short-term sales. If there is no difference between the two brand shares (STAS is exactly 100 and ADIMPACT is zero), the campaign 'has no effect'. If the indices are high, then the campaign is creating sales (but remember possible promotion and Purchase/Viewing associations!).

By 1994[24] Reichel could quote from 167 case histories analysed over two years. His findings were very similar to Jones' smaller sample summarised at the same conference. As we saw above, he added an important dimension which Jones did not study: 'Sales response diminishes as more time passes since exposure to the commercial.' In other words, he found a bigger share lift when he looked at ad exposures a single day before the purchase than when he counted exposures over 28 days – he was rediscovering adstock. He also found that decay varied with brand circumstances.

A-to-S Impact have also published[25] how they can advise about schedules. For an individual brand they give an example of a table of 'sales effects' at different numbers of 'at least' OTS in various time intervals before a purchase occasion. Here is an extract from a typical table, showing percentage increases in brand share:

	1 day before	up to 7 days before
1+ OTS	23	13
2+ OTS	27	17

The longer the interval, it is likely that the most recent OTS was longer ago, leading to a smaller effect (13 is smaller than 23). This overcomes the fact that there are probably more OTS to have an effect. More OTS do produce a better result (27 is larger than 23).

For an individual case, the data are inevitably lumpy;[26] in applications, data for a large number of relevant brands are sensibly calculated and used. Further, for each brand, the effects of price, promotion and weight of TV viewing by the shopper have been removed by co-variance. Thus, an array of data is available which predicts the effects of both decay and diminishing returns. That it is a set of numbers, rather than a formula, makes no difference to its usefulness as a benchmark.

One of the implications is that 'frequency provides spread: higher levels increase the likelihood that an exposure will occur close to the purchase occasion'. Another is that unlike STAS the system takes into account, to a certain extent, the earlier OTS. Complex planning issues are not over-simplified, nor are 'easy-to-apply, formula-based courses of action' recommended.

It is now possible to start with the likely cover distribution each week from a proposed schedule. Then find the resulting percentage increases predicted by the array above (making the assumption that these are unbiased estimates). Apply these to a base sales forecast (without ad effects). In this way the user of the system can play war games, trying out different schedules and seeing the predicted improvement in sales. Seasonality is built in this way: the percentage increase when the base is high produces a bigger result.

In an example, a traditional flighted schedule of two five-week bursts and one four-week burst was compared with the same 14 weeks advertising distributed carefully across the year, both at 55 ratings a week, and with a modified continuous schedule all year, averaging 15 ratings a week.

The added sales over the year for the original schedule are +3.6 per cent, against +4.6 per cent for the redistributed weeks and +4.8 per cent for modified continuous schedule. Although the bursts were well placed, against good value weeks, diminishing returns reduced the advertising effect. The same rate per week over more widely spaced weeks prevented this; so did reducing the ratings per week (though there may be 'possible concerns about running at drastically lowered levels').

The method has many of the features of the CV-DD model, and the evaluation of the schedules looks to me very similar to what BAT (in Chapter 7) would do. The use of an array, rather than formulae for decay and diminishing returns, is ingenious; the problem of selecting the 'relevant' brand data to create the array is analogous to picking the parameters for the systems in Chapter 7. The need to create all the weekly cover data for the schedule is presumably not too arduous on the computer.

Erwin Ephron and recency

Erwin Ephron started work with A.C.Nielsen. His trade was learned at BBDO and Carl Ally, but his greatest learning experience was gained running his own advertising agency – one which (in the 1970s) billed $150 million. This got him away from research and media and as he says he then 'saw media as the advertiser sees it'.

Eventually he set up a consultancy, specialising in media planning. He was fortunately hired by S.C.Johnson to evaluate the approach of their media director, Gus Priemer. Priemer took Ephron through the internal memos in which he had set out his then controversial views, and which he later developed into a book.[27] This quote from it might almost be an explanation of recency:

One exposure, at the right time, may also be enough to allow an interested consumer to accept the brand on the basis of its advertising. If this is correct, the only function of what we know as 'frequency' is to provide this one exposure often enough to reach all potential acceptors at the right point in time. ... The right time (is) the last exposure to advertising immediately prior to consumer purchase in this product category ... immediately following a problem.

His example is seeing the first cockroach of the year, and going to the store to buy roach killer.

Ephron's eyes were opened by these ideas. Priemer believed advertising was to remind, not to teach – the weak theory again. To him, the idea of effective frequency was irrelevant.

Sources of recency planning

Another influence, as for many, was Herb Krugman. Ephron has set out what he learned in a tribute[28] which was part of a historical review series. Krugman was misinterpreted, says Ephron, as seems to be the fate of all media research pioneers. His disciples read his key paper as a scheduling model, to be applied to the *number of exposures*. It must be admitted this was an easy mistake, as the paper contains phrases of ambiguous meaning. But he was describing three *stages* an individual may go through when meeting an advertising campaign: 'What is it?', 'What of it?' and 'the true reminder'. Or, according to Ephron, 'curiosity, recognition and decision'.

Ephron cites Krugman as the father of recency planning. He quotes a key sentence in his 1992 review, when he had fully realised the importance of what Krugman actually said.

The large budget is powerful because, like a product sitting on a shelf, you never know when the consumer is looking for you, so you have to rent the shelf space the whole time. And, advertising (is) powerful only when the viewer is interested'.

What we should aim at is presence, or share of front-of-mind, not frequency in the sense of repetition. Hence one of Ephron's key expositions[29] of his approach contains in the title a further tribute:

More weeks, less weight: the shelf-space model of advertising, with the sub-head, *Advertising needs continuity, because not being there with a message is like being out-of-stock.*

He might well have quoted from a remarkable paper by Leo Bogart[30] and others, which preceded Krugman's. This attacks the assumption that 'those messages which leave virtually no discernible memory trace at all may, through the force of repetition, turn out to have a residual effect'. Not only could a single OTS have a measurable response, but it did so 'on the very few people who were already (whether they knew it or not) ready to buy'. Hence, 'frequent coverage of all the potential customers is the way (to make the customer jump).'

This argument against repetition, and in favour of a single OTS on those who are in the market at the time, was based on an experiment in newspapers. Perhaps because the medium was not television, the lesson seems not to have been much noticed.

Echoing Bogart's title,[31] Lawrence Gibson reported recently on 63 marketplace experiments carried out between 1976 and 1985. General Mills placed TV ads so that shoppers were exposed to a single OTS for a particular brand. In a telephone interview, the key question asked was the offer of a price-off coupon for any brand in the category. This was taken to measure the effect of the ad seen the evening before. A high response was typically that 5.1 per cent asked for the advertised brand after seeing the ad, and only 1.6 per cent among those who could not have seen it.

The main conclusion is about the potential effect of a single opportunity to see, although this is the 'minority theory'. This is another of the papers cited by Ephron as backing for recency planning. Gibson also found that the gains were variable and unpredictable. More spend on copy and copy research was indicated, as General Foods had concluded years before.

In the early 1990s, the word used by Ephron was 'propinquity'. The ad had to be near the purchase occasion. When asked by Procter and Gamble for a view on flighting, his ideas crystallised. He found that Jim Van Cleave of P&G used the word 'recency' for the same idea, and Ephron recognised its aptness (and client use!). By the mid-1990s 'recency planning' was established.[32] Ephron now calls the approach the 'mainstream' for fast-moving packaged goods and he is sure that considered-purchase categories will follow.

By the late 1990s it had been tested by enough advertisers in the US (including Procter and Gamble, Coca-Cola, Kraft, General Mills, Pfizer and Warner-Lambert) to have proven benefits. There is no doubt that in-market tests are the convincing way to support theory. It is possible, however, that the brands involved are mostly those for which the VC-DD model would recommend modified continuity anyway, in which case this is not evidence for universal applicability.

The confidence felt by Ephron in 1996 was enough for him to write a very critical review[33] of the Association of National Advertisers' book, *Advertising Reach and Frequency*, which I covered in Chapter 10. These comments are worth reading for the insights into the confusion the industry suffered and which I also described in the last chapter.

Support for recency

The reader has by now learned what the recency approach is. To summarise further an already simple argument (simplicity is one of its greatest strengths), it is based on the universe of purchase decisions, not on the universe of viewers. These decisions are about *which brand* to buy, not *whether to buy* a product in the category. For most categories, some shoppers are in the market every day. Advertising effects decay rapidly, the ad you saw last has greatest influence. Yours should be the ad last seen – for every purchase. So the budget should be spread thinly; continuity is efficient; flights are wasteful because of the losses to competitors when you are off air.

This is the sort of argument to which a first reaction is, 'Of course!' Ephron calls it 'a sharply-drawn picture with energy'. It requires little additional work from the planner – the idea of continuity (at some minimum rate, like 60 ratings a week) is easy to apply.

It is the conclusion Jones also promulgates, though Ephron stresses the scheduling implications more. Ephron quotes him (sometimes uncritically, in my view) and Reichel in support. Ephron is, primarily, both a practitioner and a theorist, not an analyst or experimentalist. Data are not the essence of his argument, though he uses the analyses of others to back his case. His contribution to the debate on the right analyses for single-source data is that 'it serves no purpose commensurate with the heat it generates'.

I see Ephron's argument as relevant to a lot of brands. In fact, we have published[34] a statement of the points on which we agree, and where we disagree. My questions are: Does recency apply to all situations? What do we do about the others? Is the day-to-day application of the idea the same as Ephron's disciples assume? In practice, what modifications are allowed and how are they to be agreed?

The case for recency in my terms

In Chapter 7 we saw that what I call the Jones-Ephron situation does indeed call for 'modified-continuous' scheduling. In order to explain this, I need to go through the components of the problem as I have defined it, with Ephron's position as I see it.

I begin my description of a scheduling job with the *costs* to be paid at different times. Ephron is very well aware that costs must be taken into account. He gives no explicit advice (except, presumably, in individual consultation) about how to do so, except that it is in high-cost periods we should be off air, unless the budget is adequate for us to be literally continuous.

Once (recently) is enough

He does advise publicly that category seasonality should be used to modify a strictly uniform schedule. Again, he does not spell out explicitly how these or other *values* should be used, other than to be on air when there is a lot of shopping. For both cost and value hiatuses, it is the reach threshold which dictates for how much of the year we should be on and off air.

He assumes rapid *decay*. In general, OTS earlier than a week before brand choice are ignored. For large budgets (he quotes McDonald's) he recommends an even shorter period – half a week or a day.

Ehpron explains the neglect of possible *long-term effects* in three ways. First, by an argument similar to Keynes' 'In the long run we are all dead'. Specifically, he says, 'Recency focuses on immediate effects, because they help keep the brand in business', and 'If you don't get enough next purchases, building a brand won't matter'. The argument is practical and appealing, but I would hate it to be true that all advertisers concentrate exclusively on the short term.

Second, there is a measurement problem. You get no credit, in modern businesses, for contributions which have no numbers attached. Until accepted methods quantify convincing long-term benefits, scheduling for the long term will go unrewarded. This is a realistic view, if again a depressing one.

Finally, he believes long-term effects are usually clearly signalled by short-term ones. If a campaign works, that is, it produces repeat sales, you see this fast.

He assumes *diminishing returns* are always steep, but has never said that additional exposures produce no returns.

The *cover criterion* is therefore simple: aim at maximum reach or one plus cover. The media execution is called 'continuous reach': 'Always plan short-term reach, never plan frequency', 'Select media by cost per reach point, starting with the lowest cost', 'By adding weeks, recency produces more weekly reach points across the year'.

Reactions to recency

Some planners wince when they see a near-continuous schedule with, what seems to them, remarkably few ratings each week. The reassurance of a concentrated attack has been taken away. High peaks in the tracking study scores are unlikely. They experience discomfort in three ways: 'Won't I lose frequency, the good results of three or more hits, high response to high pressure?', 'Won't I have lower cover in my reporting periods, say, four weeks?' and 'How can one exposure be enough?'

Ephron's reply reminds us that we are allocating scarce resources. He does not claim that one exposure is 'enough', only that diminishing returns mean that later exposures are worth less than the first. Of course a second exposure *here* would increase frequency and pressure; yes, it would gain some sales – but more sales will be lost by not being *there*.

The defenders of flights and bursts seem to concentrate on the good results while on air. Like three-card tricksters, they are diverting your attention from the bad results when off air. They point out the high pressure and cover during reporting periods, but not that they have fewer reporting periods.

Ephron says that the easiest sales to influence are those caught by the first OTS in a short period like a week or less. Concentrate on the easy sales and sacrifice the harder ones. This is a 'skimming' strategy and is the essence of recency planning.

He also says, 'recency planning does not eliminate frequency. Frequency is the result of the sum of exposures over weeks.' In other words, you still get the repeated exposures on the same people, they are just more spread out. Anyway, they 'are better thought of as presence, not as repetition'.

It seems to me that we are back to different interpretations of Zielske (see again Figure 5.4, p. 63). If you really want a high pressure for some reason, you do not see the spread-out exposures as equally valuable, because you know you do not get your peak. Here is where the tracking study point comes in. When you are set a target, you need your ad effect to peak in order to reach it. If this is your position, as with Naples in 1979, you want an 'adequate response', then you are ready to pay the price of diminishing returns. Ephron's position is that the overall response, not the peak, is higher with a continuous schedule.

The second question, about the cover criterion, is also answered by the 'spreading-out' argument. You do actually get the high-cover criterion you want; that is, if targeting and buying are sufficiently skilful. You just get it over a longer time.

Proper discussion on these and similar points seems to me impossible without actual input for a VC-DD model. Ephron understands very well the importance of value and cost. He chooses not to emphasise the irregularities of this background, in order to concentrate on decay and diminishing returns. If value and cost are constant, I showed in Chapter 7 that continuity is indeed the best policy, but it is only clearly so when decay is fast and diminishing returns are steep. Otherwise there is little difference between the two scheduling strategies. In real life, values and costs do indeed vary and we can take advantage of this, but only if we allow modifications to strict continuity.

I often arrive at a schedule Ephron would approve of. But often decay and diminishing returns are not so steep, and variations in values and costs are significant. Then the balance goes the other way, and flighting or bursts are preferable.

Shorter lengths, other media

Ephron's enthusiasm for recency has led him to argue[29] for changes to spot length ('the shelf-space model encourages 15s'), cheaper dayparts and channels ('shifting money from Prime to Day, to syndications, cable and unwired networks') and other media ('monthly magazines and radio').

He knows these are not purely media decisions. The schedules may be better, but this has to be balanced against the quality or sales-effectiveness of the lower-cost options. There are no general rules here, only choices which are part of campaign decisions. Media may propose alternatives, it does not dispose.

I mentioned in Chapter 2 the way magazine scheduling differs from TV. Ephron has gone more deeply[35] into the differences, challenging some print-planning traditions.

He sees a problem in expectations from the two media: TV, he says, is thought to be for short-term effects, while print works more gradually. This is more of an American view than a British one. He says the evidence does not support the expectation, and that if print were planned as an immediate-effect medium it would work that way. Magazines have simply become a poor relation in which advertisers under-invest creatively, in both research and dollars. Print schedules are seen as background, instead of being allowed to justify themselves in the same way as TV.

Ephron's contributions

Ephron has made two great contributions. First, because he is a respected and practical planner, and his message circulates in media circles, he has been able to change received wisdom. Reichel has told me about his relief in having allies for the short-term point of view: 'I mean, we could feel the change ... something like a sharp increase in room temperature.' The norm for large advertisers in the US is now different.

Where half-lives are short, shoppers' purchase decisions are frequent and advertising is mainly a reminder, this change is beneficial.

Second, he has put forward the weak theory of advertising in a specially convincing way. He says,

Stop thinking that an opportunity to see causes a purchase. It is the empty box causes the purchase, but only by telling you to buy something. You

need more cereal, more gasoline, a new refrigerator. If the 'box' held a product you enjoyed, you might re-purchase it.

But if your repertoire includes other brands, recent OTS influence brand choice. On these particular buyers who are actually about to shop, the OTS work in a forceful way. Overall, advertising works feebly by comparison, simply because most viewers are not in the market at the time.

I see Ephron's simplifications as a rhetorical device. Without them, he would not have had his profound effect on current practice. Doubtless he discusses with clients how to modify literal continuity. Readers saw in Chapter 7 how necessary this can be. My own belief is that the real task is now to identify and deal with the many exceptions.

12   Other multivariate work

Introduction

We all want to know how big our advertising effects are, how long they last, whether there are diminishing returns and so on. But our view is obscured by all the other factors affecting sales. There can be many of these, so the situation is *multi*variate. In this chapter, all the methods described take this point fully into account. The work becomes more realistic, but at the cost of complexity.

There are three sorts of data used to investigate the situation, and all of these appear here: pure single source, fused purchase and media panels, and normal time series data. Most of the investigations reported are by other analysts and all took place after Jones, Reichel and Ephron had made the recommendations reported in the last chapter.

Reactions to when ads work

Criticisms and suggestions for improvements soon began.[1] They clustered round the two points already made. The first suggestion was: are there particular factors affecting the general sales share which might be confounded with shoppers' exposure to our advertising? The second, and raised less often: can we accept STAS without a check on possible Purchase/Viewing bias across individuals? Then, if these problems arise, how to cope with them? Finally, what implications are there for scheduling?

These are difficult questions, and a variety of answers were developed during this renaissance of interest in single source. They did not affect the admiration aroused by Jones' raising of these issues, or for his separate arguments that the effects of promotions on the long-term good of the brand are usually dubious, and on other points.

It was noted with regret that the data Jones had used were not available to anyone else. The normal way to settle differences is to share common data, discuss their implications and to try out different hypotheses and analyses in the hope of agreement. The only people who could advance the discussion seriously were those with their own data. This was frustrating to others, who could put up only hypotheses.

Jones was in great demand as a speaker and consultant. From this period he reports a very revealing story about advertising people, that the media head of a leading American agency thought his conclusions were counter-intuitive. 'I think what he meant was that my facts seemed to run counter to his prejudices.' However, this agency later changed its mind.

In 1996 Nielsen organised a conference in Sydney, Australia, at which Jones was the main speaker. In many ways, the meeting was a repetition of the American seminars on effective frequency: misunderstandings about definitions, and disputes which were not resolved. It was more positive in that some new analyses of direct relevance were reported; some of these contributions were rewritten in later papers described below. His own lecture was described as a *tour de force*[2] – he thrives on the podium. His response to questions on technique was that he deals only in facts; he is not interested in theory. STAS is undoubtedly a 'fact' – it is a number produced by a specified procedure. So are the numbers of choices of our brand at no OTS, one OTS and so on. Debates are not about the reality of these numbers, but about the claim that they describe only the direct effects of advertising.

The two other senior speakers suggested other issues. Naples pointed out that competitors' advertising was not taken into account. He speculated, as he had written earlier, that more research would show that each brand has its own response function. McDonald raised the possible effects of earlier advertising and the fact that brand switching was not investigated. He pointed out that STAS can be decomposed into the two indices he had used himself: Change and Repeat.

Do Nielsen's analyses corroborate Jones?

In Germany, A.C.Nielsen pursued the analyses started by Jones and described briefly in Chapter 11. It was evident to the company before too long that more was needed, but for some time it was unclear how to proceed.

I proposed to them two ways to improve on STAS. First, I designed a simple way into the data, one which market researchers are used to – straightforward descriptions of the relationships between pairs of explainers. With a table for each variable, and a column of all the other variables down one side, it was easy to look at brand shares for combinations of any two variables as well as for each single variable. Thus, the association of brand share with price or with recent advertising (defined by adstock at various half-lives, or by OTS in the week before purchase) could be looked at. Also, by *both* price *and* advertising. These contingency tables are easy to use, and they give quick insights into probable associations.

But the best sort of analysis, I thought, was the full multivariate approach we developed which is outlined below. AC.Nielsen, however, decided to develop its own model. In return for our proposals, we got access to some of the data, which was a valuable step for us.

Nielsen's development was in two stages. First, a move to logistic regression of a single brand choice, allowing for loyalty, socio-demographics, the brand's and its competitors' advertising and promotions. Then in 1997 it announced[3] a model developed with Unilever, called BCQ (Brand Choice and Quantity) in which all competitive cross-effects were allowed for (each brand was compared against each of the others).

This was specifically to correct STAS for advertising exposures (ours and competitors') earlier than the seven-day interval. A half-life of seven days is given as an example. They found 'because marketing managers and retailers tend to co-ordinate promotional and advertising activities', it was necessary to disentangle promotional effects. The loyalty of an individual to the brand was calculated – 'the basic probability of purchases without (other) influences'. Distribution was also allowed for.

Thus A.C.Nielsen in Germany has moved a long way from the US analyses in the early 1990s described in Chapter 11.

Do IRI analyses corroborate Jones?

In 1996, IRI used BehaviorScan data[4] to check what STAS actually measured. At this time the use of single-source data for media planning was falling out of fashion. On that front, 'things have been quiet for the past couple of years', said Gary Schroeder. He attributed this to disagreements on how it should be used, the supporters and the detractors having reached stalemate.

Schroeder welcomed Jones' revival of advertising effects measurement, though he felt the actual index was not yet independently validated. Data 'as-they-fall' may not give a pure measure, and the possible interference of promotions was the factor he singled out. Suppose the advertiser plans his advertising to coincide with promotion peaks – a common policy, as A.C.Nielsen pointed out. If the promotions are effective, STAS may be large for this reason alone.

Schroeder and his colleagues picked seven media weight tests where the reasons for sales changes had been established experimentally. They calculated STAS for the same data, both from purchase occasions (the official definition) and by comparing volume shares rather than occasion shares, which corresponded closely.

Overall, the BehaviorScan estimate of advertising's effect was close to STAS in two cases, but not in the other five. In six out of the seven cases they found that STAS was related to the proportion of the brand sold on promotion each week – and to competitive promotions in the other direction.

Since loyalty to the brand is 'the largest factor in brand choice', Schroeder suggested that some way needs to be found to control the calculations for it – as well as promotions, weight of viewing and so on. The need to allow for other possible causes of the number observed is now a normal comment and the question today is how, rather than whether it is necessary.

Methods were described to redefine the index. 'The promise of this work demonstrates that a more comprehensive and robust STAS measure can be built to measure advertising ... Controls are needed to account for the effects of loyalty, merchandising and consumer promotions.'

Further comments[5] from an off-shoot of BehaviorScan in Germany were given by Raimund Wildner of the German company GfK, speaking with Klaus Kindelman of MGM at a conference in Paris in 1997. Their data came from a panel of 1,000 households in Hassloch. Following BehaviorScan practice, the shoppers used special cards for their purchases in seven major stores. Promotions going on in these stores were known. The viewing in these households was also known, via a meter on the TV set. Advertising transmission data were added to make the MediaScan panel data complete.

Wildner and Kindelman thought the definition of ad exposure was rather arbitrary at seven days, and would have preferred this to be varied to investigate the time effect. Heavier viewers are demographically different and contribute more to the ad-exposed group – they may also shop different-ly (and, I would add, often do). Competitors' advertising had been wrongly ignored. Promotions can be a very important influence and may take place at the same time as the campaign.

The technique used to estimate the size of these three interferences was co-variance analysis, which estimates the effect of each possible confounding factor.

In one example given, the raw STAS for the brand was 117, but, when the other factors had been allowed for, the 'adjusted' STAS was 104. The largest part of the reduction was due to promotions and the next largest (and negative, of course) was competitors' advertising. In another example, adjusted STAS was larger than raw STAS because the Purchase/Viewing bias was negative and had pulled down the original observed effect.

Because Jones continued to defend STAS and also attacked[6] some IRI findings, a response[7] from Leonard Lodish summarised the US Behavior-Scan analyses: 'more than 75 per cent of the variation in BehaviorScan results is not associated with STAS.' He also pointed out the reasons again. 'STAS assumes that all the differences between the exposed and non-exposed groups are due to the sales impacts of the brand's TV exposures', neglecting possible effects from deals, features, display and pricing. Further, 'what if the exposed group was more likely to purchase the brand because they had purchased it more in the past (possibly because of past advertising exposures)?' So, 'is it fair to credit this week's TV ad exposure for this week's brand sales to the household?'

The Jones-Lodish debate has continued,[8] neither side convincing the other. Jones strengthened his defence of STAS from 'resembles an experiment' to 'two samples which are similar in all respects except one – the inclusion or absence of the variable to be tested. This is of course the classic methodology of the controlled experiment'. He therefore sees comparison with BehaviorScan to be meaningless.

Lodish, correctly in my view, points out that STAS 'differs from the controlled experiment in very important ways'. Nothing has been done to recognise or control differences in past exposures. If current buyers have been targeted by media planners, why should advertising be credited for sales that were there anyway (this point could have been expanded to include the unwitting targeting of heavy viewers, and because of Purchase/Viewing bias the result may be fewer sales or more sales). 'Promotion, distribution, shelf placement, competitive activity and in-store conditions' are not adjusted for, week by week, for those exposed and not exposed to advertising.

An associate of BehaviorScan, GfK, set up a French single-source panel in Angers with Médiamétrie. While a case study has been published,[9] 'it is much too early (in 1996) to confirm such conclusions (about the shape of response), or the works of Erwin Ephron and John Philip Jones'.

I quote the A.C.Nielsen and BehaviorScan-inspired papers at some length to show the interest and new thinking which Jones had sparked. There are other examples.[10]

Applications to scheduling

The Myers report, *Managing Media Options,* published in March 1998, is primarily about TV buying. It covers subjects like the inventory on offer in the US (channels, dayparts, programs and so on), the ways these reach specific targets economically with an agreed 'effective frequency' (or by weighting OTS in some way). It also covers the methods for selecting the best options. Thus, it includes what I have called here 'buying', over shorter periods than the time I have taken as the period for planning decisions. Its starting point is that the availability of raw TV panel data means there are better ways of defining a good schedule than 'simple gross rating points'.

It must be true that adding explainers, such as reach, to ratings will improve fits to marketplace data. They also add to the complexity of scheduling, in that in addition to ratings these explainers also have to be forecast. I believe 'simple gross ratings points' are the primary explainer. Other measures are useful and may be added, as explained in Chapter 6. But we should never lose sight of ratings because, as boxers say, 'A good big 'un will always beat a good little 'un'.

The Myers Report adds the comments that a media plan 'must embrace the entire marketing mix' and therefore take into account the 'new science of marketing mix modelling ... which is fairly new to ad agencies', and so 'sales effectiveness modelling (is) the next generation'.

Apart from the word 'new' I agree with this. A sound schedule is one based on a correct understanding of how advertising works for the brand. As the report points out, there are two benefits. First, as we learn more, we can plan better. Second, the demonstration of advertising benefits encourages brand management to invest in media advertising, sometimes today at the expense of promotions. The examples of Kraft and Campbell Soup are quoted.

The report gives prominence to the acquisition in 1997 by Carat (a media planning and buying specialist) of Media Marketing Assessment (MMA – a marketing consulting firm). Some of MMA's findings and techniques have been published.[11] Marketing mix modelling and the allocation of the budget to marketing activities are included, but it is scheduling that is of more concern here.

'Smart Scheduler' uses modelling findings to allocate funds across weeks, major markets in the US, and channels. Some factors, now familiar to the reader, appear in the list of considerations in scheduling: budget and costs of course, but also category and brand seasonality, decay (carry over) and saturation (diminishing returns), reach and frequency goals, promotion calendar, competitive activity and differences between markets (regions). The method is similar to the '520 cells' generalised hill-climbing outlined in Chapter 8 for a stepwise allocation for 52 weeks and ten regions.

The criteria used are analysed simultaneously while the system is building a schedule. ... It allocates advertising weight to the week that maximises incremental advertising-driven volume and meets the criteria you have added ... until it has exhausted your budget. ... This results in schedules that consistently deliver more short-term advertising volume for your brand. In tests, the increase in ad-driven volume has ranged from 6 per cent to over 25 per cent higher than non-optimised schedules.

Other firms have been modelling and using the results in scheduling for some years. The UK consultancy OHAL, founded by the innovator Callaghan O'Herlihy, was first active in the 1970s. Its representation of advertising pressure[12] includes a 'trigger' device.

The international research company Millward Brown modelled awareness for many years, as described in Chapter 4, and then moved into sales modelling.[13] This has recently resulted in advice on scheduling. Again, 'FORCE' modelling uses more than rating points as the television measure. Cover is introduced, in a complex way, as an explainer. I give a very brief description[14] of this model, some findings, and then some resulting comment on schedules.

Advertising is now represented by the distribution of frequencies of exposure: a number of viewers had exactly one OTS in a particular week, other viewers had two and so on. Each group is reduced as time passes – for example, if 50 people saw the ad once in week 1, it is assumed only 45 are still affected in week 2 (if the decay rate is 10 per cent per week). But the groups are also added to if there is further advertising. Thus 'decayed frequencies' are calculated. These are 'regarded as effective frequencies'.

The argument for using a cover or reach criterion can be strong in extreme cases. Millward Brown quotes an example of an advertiser shifting the target definition from 'mothers' to 'mothers watching in children's viewing time'. The same number of ratings on mothers were bought, but effectiveness fell. A cover figure would have revealed the drop as not all mothers watch at this time. In fact the researchers were led to their work with cover by seeing changes in awareness due solely to buying changes, not in the advertising. Up to 10 per cent improvement in return, due to careful media planning, has been measured in marketplace experiments.

Response need not be linear. Diminishing returns are used mainly to model awareness, but the method is increasingly applied to sales and image data. The 'FORCE' parameter is identical to the parameter F in Chapter 5: if the first OTS creates 20 per cent awareness, the second increases[15] this to 36 per cent. This reduction is applied to the decayed frequencies and the total is then created.

Apart from this treatment of cover, modified as explained both for decay and diminishing returns, the model covers the usual factors explaining the dependent variable. It is carried out regionally when possible. Possible long-term effects are studied by comparing the movement of the base level (in actual awareness or sales, less the short-term effects) with the advertising input. This involves 'a lot of assumptions', for example, about the possible results of other factors, but an advertising effect can then be estimated.

Because over 60 sales models have now been constructed, in the US and Europe, some generalisations are possible. There is a wide variety of sizes of effect – a factor of 20 between effective and ineffective advertising is estimated. Only 14 per cent of the examples showed a clear economic return from short-term effects. Being in a big category is the strongest condition for this, for obvious reasons – the costs per thousand are spread over more purchases. Product launches, brands that had not been advertised before and promotional support are also good indicators. The additional economic benefit from the long term is probably much higher – up to ten or even 20 times as large.

The main finding, as the reader of Chapters 5 and 7 would expect, is that F varies across campaigns, and the higher F is, the closer to continuity the plan should be. The key use of the model is to help set burst sizes and maximum ratings per week, in order to 'avoid preaching to the converted'. It is said that for high F there is a danger of over-spending, and that in some cases a budget reduction is possible. Awareness can be predicted by the model, and the maximum level and average value can be calculated for different schedules.

A personal solution for single-source modelling

The second time I tackled single-source data, after my failure in Chicago, I realised I needed a new model. Its components have already been outlined, but more important was the way it was used. Up to then, single-source data had always been reduced to a few summary tables. Analysts had been blinded by its singularity. In normal circumstances, we do not expect to look at a large body of data about different campaigns and conclude 'Advertising has such-and-such effect on average'. We know that sometimes it has large effects, sometimes small, and we look at brands individually. I decided to develop methods to look at a few cases in depth, and not to attempt an average over many cases.

The list of influences must start with *average behaviour*. We shall see the short-term blips in sales only as differences from this norm. For the individual shopper, this meant her overall loyalty to our brand. McDonald saw the importance of allowing for something of the kind when he compared the shopper's current decision with what she chose last time. But why not use all the information we have about the shopper and take her average? It might have been possible to use the average for all occasions except this one, but I did not want to be so complicated (it meant 'loyalty' changing on each occasion). Instead I decided to analyse a variable which I called *buy-loyalty* (*buy* minus *loyalty*). If you choose my brand on a particular occasion, you score 1.0 – this is *buy*. If you choose my brand very occasionally – say my share of your purchases is only one in ten – then *loyalty* is 0.1. So *buy-loyalty* is +0.9, a high number, showing this is a significant positive event and that it is worth looking for the cause.

A digression

As I write this, I realise I am committing the crime of which all writers of scientific papers are guilty: after the event, making the process of discovery look like a smooth progression. This is rarely the case, so it seems worth a short digression to explain how this development actually happened.

I first tried a method of creating the contingency table which explains most of the brand-choice decision, then the next most important decision and so on. This has the impressive name 'automatic interaction detection' but, apart from confirming that loyalty was by far the most important factor, it did not reveal much, so it was abandoned.

Like others before me, I planned to explain the variable I call *buy*. One of the explainers was going to be *loyalty*. As explained above, this is one when the shopper always chooses us, zero when she never does so, and it may be any rational number in between (for example, 0.25 if she chose us one time in four).

After using this system for some time I realised there were three reasons it was not such a good idea. First, loyalty explained such a large proportion of the variability in the data that other effects were hard to see.

Second, and more importantly, my dependent variable *buy* was actually part of the explainer *loyalty*, since this purchase decision was part of the set of decisions that made up *loyalty*. Statisticians are unhappy when this happens. But *buy-loyalty* is a construct from *all* the brand-decision data, none of which are left on the explainer side of the equation, so the potential critics are disarmed.

Third, some statisticians are unhappy when the dependent variable can take only two values (0 or 1) and have invented types of regression called logit and probit to deal with this. I ran such regressions, and discovered that the programs were not in common use, that the results were presented in a form unfamiliar to most people and that the results were almost indistinguishable from ordinary regression on *buy-loyalty*.

I also dropped from the analysis shoppers who always buy our brand – or never do so. In either case, she cannot tell us anything about short-term advertising effects because she always behaves the same way, irrespective of our activities. It is useful to know how many such shoppers there are, but no more.

Finally, if the Purchase/Viewing index affects STAS, as seen in Chapter 11, does it not also affect the estimate made by this regression? No, because the regression is looking at a *difference* in behaviour, the one between what she does this time and what she normally does, described by her loyalty. It is the association between loyalty and average advertising exposure which is measured by the Purchase/Viewing index. *Buy-loyalty* has escaped from any bias this creates.

The simple words, 'I decided to analyse a variable I called *buy-loyalty*' conceal the doubts, false trails and midnight oil. This stage of an analysis consists of part back to the drawing board, part tuning an engine. It certainly does not involve making decisions which were obvious at the time. Doubtless most of the discoveries in these chapters are of this type.

Thus the method I recommend[16] is a standard least-squares regression – but using variables which are some trouble to create from the raw panel data. It takes full account of the other influences on sales – such as loyalty, relative price, promotions, distribution if it is available and other store-level activities, plus competitors' advertising as well as our own. It examines different rates of decay and, similarly, different diminishing returns. It can also take into account interactions between variables, such as advertising during periods of promotion or low price.

I realised that the same data could give us the normal weekly figures we were used to getting from separate purchasing and media panels. I analyse these too, using existing adstock methods. This may look like a backwards step, but answers the interesting question – how different, or how much better, are the answers when we use the power of single source? If the improvement is small, perhaps the extra trouble and expense is not worthwhile? The weekly data also allow additional analyses, which are not available from the occasions data: descriptive plots and the calculations of Consumer Brand Equity.

Don't forget variety!

The preceding examples of modelling, including some of my own, have used aggregate data; results on all shoppers are treated in total. In the last section of this chapter, where fused viewing and purchase data are used, some examples are given of the variety concealed by the totals.

I have already commented on the danger of reporting results only as an average across a number of different campaigns. A suggested set of three dimensions by which campaigns are likely to differ was given[17] in 1997. Admittedly, this is a comment on effective frequency, but it can also be read as applying to any schedule evaluation. The three dimensions are:
- *brand familiarity*, since it is likely a campaign works differently for a brand we know little about and one we know well,
- *message complexity*, since the communication and effect of something simple cannot be the same as one which takes repetition to appreciate, and
- *message novelty*, which is a similar point to brand familiarity.

The other main kind of variety lies with the viewers and shoppers. This is not the familiar breakdown by light to heavy, used many times in this book, but by usage of the advertisement. A survey[18] concluded that an OTS can

indeed 'work effectively using just one or two exposures'. But – it depends on who you ask. Four groups of respondent were identified:
–   some are highly interested in the product and will respond rapidly;
–   some are less interested and repetition is needed to prompt them to action;
–   some ignore the campaign, irrespective of frequency,
–   and a few will pretend in research to respond even though they have not seen the ad at all.

Finally, a sensible point[19] is made by two New Zealand researchers about the data needed to investigate who responds to TV advertising and with what exposure.

They admit that pure single-source research is the Holy Grail – the ideal source. This is where the same respondents tells us about shopping and viewing. However, these panels are expensive, and, as experts have assured me, difficult to make a profit on. To merge data from two sources, or as AGB have done in New Zealand and Australia, to add a product consumption diary to an existing viewing and reading panel, is to approximate to the ideal, and at an acceptable price.

Entry of an operational researcher

In Chapter 11, I described the simple contingency tables used by Jones and Reichel to estimate advertising effects in single-source panels. Andrew Roberts has used tables of this type for the same purpose, but more carefully. His approach is another example of multivariate analysis applied to disentangling the complexities of real data.

Roberts carries out this work as Technical Director of Taylor Nelson Sofres in London. He came to this interest and to this position in the same roundabout way as all of us, but in his case it is easier to see the relevance of an important step.

After he took a BSc. in Aeronautical Engineering he joined the team working on the Harrier jump-jet at Hawker Siddeley. There is a small piece of the aircraft flying today which he designed. In those days, engineering meant a lot of repeated and approximate calculations. I remember keeping, like Roberts, a slide rule in my jacket pocket. Eventually this became tedious and Roberts looked for a new career. To train for it, Roberts took an MSc. in Operations Research at the Cranfield Institute of Technology.

Roberts and I have discussed the high promise from this discipline at the time – and its potential application to many problems in media and advertising research. He worked first at Gallaher's, and then at the London agency of Masius Wynne-Williams. He expected to learn much, as Naples did at Levers, from experiments; he thought that models would be used more in scheduling and other allocations. All three of us were disappointed.

One of the lessons of the war, when operational research was applied to important problems, was that they should be treated as important, and given the necessary resources. This is not the same as a few neat techniques being used as the only solution for equally complex but relatively trivial difficulties. The lack of support and of seriousness in advertising applications showed in several ways.

In scheduling, for example, quite sophisticated methods had been developed 30 years ago. They never became part of the culture. Only a few specialists had the necessary training and equipment. Ordinary planners and buyers did not want to be de-skilled, and did not frequent the specialists. If the workers did not actually revolt and smash the new mechanical looms which were putting them out of work, the fear of replacement was palpable. Soon the technicians were sidelined and finally they were moved out.

There is a more complex objection, which I raised in Chapter 7. Any mechanical method, especially one which does not contain all the safeguards and unspoken rules of thumb which media people absorb, is in danger of getting out of hand. A racing car is a fine thing; it is not wise to put it on the open road under the imperfect control of a learner driver. There are genuine difficulties in combining power and sophistication with down to earth practicality.

Roberts feels that all good ideas get recycled, and that the time for powerful but non-intuitive methods may be coming round again; some are recorded in this book.

Another single-source panel

For Roberts, modelling the effects of advertising, and designing allocation models, were his first jobs. But at the agency these soon merged into day-to-day account planning. When he left, in 1987, he had overall responsibility for media and research.

At AGB, he returned to behavioural data, and to what he saw as the acid test – commercial relevance. The more emotive and certainly more subjective issues surrounding normal advertising work were losing their appeal for him. The panels which AGB ran and those they developed turned out to be a fertile field for his talents. The two most relevant to this story are now described. The first, MediaSpan, was created by a fusion process between the AGB 10,000 homes national panel (Superpanel) and the BARB TV audience panel. Purchasing housewives are given imputed estimates of their weekly exposures to a brand's advertising. The second is TVSpan; here 750 housewives in the purchasing panel in the Meridian region were equipped with TV setmeters to record the household's minute-by-minute viewing.

The fused panel is inevitably less precise in its media data, but the sample sizes are larger. More analyses have been carried out to date on this source, and these are the basis for some comments below. The true single-source panel is more precise on the time advertising is seen by shoppers, but is not large enough for many single-brand analyses. It has been used for experiments (in comparison with other Superpanel homes), and for analyses of merged brands in a single category.

Jones and Reichel adopted or devised their own indices for the apparent effect of ads recently seen; STAS and ADIMPACT are created by different calculations. Roberts approached the same two-by-two table as I described above in yet another way. The measure he finished with[20] is similar to, but not the same as, Reichel's.

Roberts considered the first table in Chapter 11 as any statistician would. The number of occasions in the 'exposed to advertising' and 'bought the brand' cell in that example is 2. What would we expect to see there, if we considered as fixed the total numbers of exposed occasions and of choices of our brand, and if there were no association between the two ways the table is split? Multiply the number of observations (6) by the proportion exposed (one half) and the proportion who bought (again one half). The result is 1.5.

It is the difference between 2 (observed) and $1\frac{1}{2}$ (expected) which matters. The ratio can be used as a measure of the effect (this gives Reichel's number), and such figures can also be used in Roberts' measure and in statistical tests of significance.

So far, you see no major difference from the previous chapter. But now comes the critical point. Roberts was well aware, from earlier work, that other factors could influence this measure and should be allowed for. He lists three in particular:
– Purchase/Viewing bias (heavy viewers may have consistently different brand shares for this brand);
– the pressure of promotions when this is simultaneous with advertising highs;
– the possibility that shoppers with different viewing habits, or different loyalties to the brand (shown in the proportion of category purchases they give to it), react differently to advertising.

This agrees with a list I have been using, except that competitors' advertising is not included. Roberts says he has not often found this of much importance, on the grounds that any one competitor's brand usually accounts for only a small proportion of total category purchases made by buyers of the advertised brand. I would add that competitors' advertising is a rather steady background in some categories. He has, however, found that the lead brand in a group of brands may influence sales of the spin-offs by its own advertising.

What is completely different is that he investigates the disturbing factors by further tables, dissecting the main table, rather than by multivariate regression which is the more usual method and of which there are examples from other analysts above. Thus, using more complex tables than Jones, he looks for advertising effects within groups of shoppers defined in relevant ways. He says[21] that 'the most obvious danger is when a natural bias exists; for example heavy TV viewers may have a greater propensity to buy the brand regardless of whether it is advertised ... the results of the contingency analysis will [otherwise] be biased in favour of advertising.' I therefore only describe the technique for one of the possible influences – the Purchase/Viewing bias. The others are dealt with in identical fashion.

Divide the occasions, by the shoppers' weights of viewing, into five equal groups. Within these, create the 2x2 tables. Carry out the same calculation of the 'expected' numbers in the key cells. The ratios of observed to expected numbers measure the advertising effects, but in their sum the disturbance due to weight of viewing has been largely removed. Further, the same statistical test of significance is available.

The process can be made a little more complex, by splitting the data into further groups, or by combining some of them. Rather than a single 'ad exposed' group, he can look at those who see just one ad, just two and so on. The point is that the whole system is under direct control, and at each step the results can be inspected and the significance estimated. The analyst learns about the complexity and interactions as the analysis proceeds.

An elegant attempt at estimating the decay of advertising effects over time is to create a 2x3 table. The first column heading is expanded from 'not exposed to advertising in the week before purchase' to 'not exposed in the 28 days before purchase' and 'exposed to advertising between 28 days and a week'. The third column is still 'exposed to advertising in the week before purchase'. Further, the 'week' in these definitions is varied, between a single day and two weeks.

Thus different effects from a day to other intervals can be compared with no short-term exposure to advertising (for four weeks). This certainly shows[22] greater effects when advertising is nearer the purchase, though there is some interference from the number of ads seen. On average, Roberts estimates a two-week half-life, which corresponds to adstock modelling findings with weekly data: 'three-quarters of the total effect are felt within a month.'

The diminishing returns which he finds have an exception. If there are several OTS within a day or so before a purchase, then there can be significantly greater response. The period over which repetition is measured matters

180

a great deal. This possibility was mentioned in Chapter 12 as a case which might require manual adjustment to a weekly produced calculated schedule.

Roberts contrasts the use of tables with regression, which is certainly more exact (the actual values are used, rather than grouping the data) but also rather mysterious. Further, regressions do not deal with interactions between the explainers in the same way. It is hard for those without any statistical training to grasp the meaning of a coefficient in a regression, while they can 'see' what a table and a ratio are telling them.

Glimpses of true complexity

The lessons from this work are mixed, in that some are simple and easily applied, while others hint at further complexity under the surface. This is a dilemma which cannot be avoided and which we met in the last chapter. How far may we simplify without over-simplifying? When is it safe to generalise and when do we sensibly reveal the tangle of interacting forces? Answering these questions is how Karl Popper describes[23] science:

> *the art of systematic over-simplification, of discerning what we may with advantage omit.*

The flexible approach to the construction of tables allows a demonstration of diminishing returns in a new way. In Chapter 5 it was the overall reaction of all the shoppers which was described. In Chapter 6 it was the individual shopper whose exposure to increasing numbers of OTS mattered. But with Roberts' technique we can take an intermediate view. We can decompose the apparent reaction of all shoppers into those of groups of shoppers by weight of viewing. McDonald has also done similar work.

For simplicity, consider only three groups – light, medium and heavy. And suppose that for each group the brand share increases *linearly* with increasing OTS. You might therefore expect that the overall reaction was also linear. But we have to take into account one fact and one reasonable possibility. The fact is that increasing weight of viewing means that from the same campaign the groups get increasing numbers of OTS. The strong possibility is that, because heavier viewers also see more competing ads, they react less to actual numbers of exposures. Hence, Roberts has suggested, some method is needed to give higher importance to OTS to lighter viewers, say, in inverse proportion to weight of viewing.

Here are hypothetical tables showing these three processes – linear response, more OTS and flatter response with increasing viewing. Also shown is total response. We reach the same conclusion as from an example in the last chapter: summing several results can give a finding which is different from the individual components.

The first table shows the percentages of viewers in each cell, totalling 100 across the rows:

OTS =	0	1	2	3	4+
Light viewers	50	40	10		
Medium viewers	30	20	20	20	10
Heavy viewers	10	10	30	30	20

The second table shows a linear response within each group, steep for light viewers and flatter for heavy viewers:

OTS =	0	1	2	3	4+
Light viewers	0	4	8		
Medium viewers	0	3	6	9	15*
Heavy viewers	0	2	4	6	11*

Response allows for 4, 5 and more OTS

Finally, the two tables are used to make the weighted overall response, from the OTS distribution in the first table and the relevant responses in the second. We get yet another surprising result from a weighted average:

OTS =	0	1	2	3	4+
Total response	0	2.4	3.2	3.6	3.7

Thus we have a demonstration that strictly linear response *within* each group is compatible with convex response *overall*. Which is 'true'? Both of them.

Which should we *use*? Roberts believes, and I agree, that the last table may mislead schedulers. Taken at face value, it suggests sharply diminishing returns. Many would conclude that it is not worth giving the total audience more than two OTS; this was indeed the interpretation suggested for similar tables in Chapter 11. The action then suggested was to build cover, to increase the 1+ OTS. But if the response within each group is linear, increasing total GRPs is more sales-effective. Two-thirds of the 4+ growth is among heavy viewers, and their sales response is still growing (linearly in this case), because we are combating competitors.

Although the example depends on the detail in contingency tables, it strengthens my belief in the validity of adstock modelling, with total ratings, on aggregate data. That can be accused of being crude, and it does deal only with 'headline' data such as overall sales and average exposure to advertising. But the aggregate model often tells us, as in Chapter 5, that the rate of diminishing returns is poorly determined and that no response function fits much better than a linear one. This may also be the correct interpretation for the deeper reason we have just seen.

More insights

Probably because Roberts works directly with groups of shoppers or of buying occasions, he is more conscious than most of the lack of homogeneity in the data. He points out, for example, that there are different sorts of repetition. Is it likely, he asks, that we will see the same effect from two OTS in a week when one was on Monday and one on Thursday – or two on Wednesday, an hour apart? Like me, he was brought up in the media tradition that concentration led to greater effects. The Wednesday pair 'should' be more effective – but we know too little about such questions.

A possible definition of a weak brand is that it has a high proportion of its sales from shoppers who give it a low proportion of their category needs. An example I have published is Hunts ketchup in the US, in contrast with Heinz. Hunts got half its sales from shoppers who gave it 40 per cent or more of their ketchup purchases; Heinz got half from shoppers who gave it 80 per cent or more. Here is another possible reason for different reactions to advertising support. Roberts' distinction between the loyalty of different shoppers allows him to look at this point too.

Such analyses shed light on the debate between the 'strong theory' (crudely, that advertising converts) and the 'weak theory' (that it reinforces, especially with product use). Roberts and I agree it is likely that the strong theory applies more to weak brands, and the weak theory to strong brands.

To spell this out: to be successful, a small brand has to gain trial and converts to increase penetration. The mechanics for a successful large brand are not the same. It is often defensive. The job of advertising is to reassure and retain its many purchasers, and to persuade only new market entrants to try what they are already partly familiar with.

Finally, Roberts has reported individual estimates of the response function, rather than an overall average. For example,[24] of 40 established brands, he found 26 with convex response and 14 with virtually linear response, where share of mind was important, rather than the absolute numbers of OTS. Of 10 new brands or re-launches, seven had linear response, one had a threshold and two were s-shaped.

Conclusions

It is possible that the long wrangles about continuity versus flighting or bursting, 'effective frequency', and even about area allocation, may be drawing to a close. Scheduling is currently getting attention for several reasons, and these have led to real improvements.

First, we have better data, better modelling and more competition between suppliers of media recommendations.

Second, there is wider recognition that to understand the contribution of advertising we have to allow for other factors as we disentangle marketplace data. The underlying models are becoming more appropriate and more realistic.

Unfortunately, but understandably, most analysts allow for only short-term effects, with possible variation in the rate of decay. A few allow for the longer-term effects, though there is not enough agreement on how this should be done.

Everyone appreciates that diminishing returns are likely to exist and are necessary in scheduling. There are various ways to allow for this.

The form of the advertising variable is not always the same: some use only ratings, others add cover in various ways.

It is likely that the differences pointed out between the various proprietary models will persist for some time, but will gradually converge as one or another approach proves more acceptable. That means, understandable and usable by non-specialists. It also means, based on a model that represents reality.

The complexity of modern television has made the computer an essential tool. The line between modelling and scheduling is blurring. Firms who model do not only explain the past, they move smoothly into recommending how to allocate new budgets.

There are still great difficulties in applying the lessons from a tiny minority of modelled brands to everyday jobs over all brands. As usual, the power will be with those who have enough data and experience to generalise with confidence and credibility. The lead will be taken by a few pioneers until the lessons become common currency and enter normal practice.

Budget, costs and values will be the backbone of every schedule. For large advertisers and established brands the allocations (across regions as well as time) are likely to be modified continually. The flesh on the bones will follow costs and values rather smoothly.

For the rest – which means the majority of planning – the decisions of when and where to support the brand will become more automated in execution, but more dependent on careful specification of the brand's needs and of the way its advertising contributes. The flesh added will grow in a more lumpy fashion, more appropriate to estimates of the decay, diminishing returns and cover appropriate to the task.

References and notes

Chapter 1

1. Broadbent, S. (1989) *The Advertising Budget*, NTC Publications Ltd.
2. 'Northland' is actually Central Scotland, and the channel studied in the first three examples is ITV.
3. See (1998) *Redefining Media Evaluation*, TSMS and Taylor Nelson Sofres.
4. Media Planning and Buying Checklist, concentrating on the TV schedule and buying criteria (see also *Spending Advertising Money*, 4th Edn., pp 393–412):

BRIEF
Administration details
Team, relevant dates, airtime budget, reporting period.

What's the brand?
Description, recent history, price, distribution, competitors...
Regional data and priorities if appropriate.

What are the business, marketing and campaign objectives?
Includes other marketing activity, its timing, and need for TV support.

Who is the TV target audience?
The real target and the buying target approximating to it.

What is the message/creative work?
Spot lengths etc.

How do we expect the advertising to work?
Discussion to help decisions on expected rate of decay, rate of diminishing returns, need for repetition.
Is there any analysis on this brand or similar brands to help these decisions?

Special factors
There are often particular events which influence timing decisions, which will affect the value we give to different weeks.
What planned activities are the advertising to support?

What expected competitors' activities are to be kept in mind?
PLANNING AND BUYING RECOMMENDATIONS
Regional allocation (if appropriate).
Schedule over weeks or months.
Cover and frequency targets
    Channel mix,
    Airtime quality.

Post-campaign reporting.

Plans to learn more about items in the brief where information is missing.

Chapter 2

1. We met Northland in Chapter 1, where it was explained I am keeping the applications non-specific. But the numbers are genuine. Viewing data are from BARB, the Broadcasters' Audience Research Board.
2. Costs are estimated in the UK by the MMS Monitor. In our two regions, housewife costs are well below the national average of £10.1 per thousand impacts, which is pulled up by the high cost in London, about £17.4. Thus for a penny you got about one housewife OTS nationally on ITV in 1997.
3. The process here is regression. The dependent variable is costs, the explainer is average ratings. R-squared was about 0.5. The residual (what is left over) is attributed here to demand.
4. The Television Audience Rating Points are averages for these cities in 1997, and for the audience of grocery buyers. The stations are the three commercial networks, also averaged, and the times are 6 a.m. to midnight.
5. *Understanding Magazine Advertising*, September 1990, and Gordon Pincott's paper *Investigating Readership Lags*, privately published by Millward Brown. I am grateful for help with this section from Alan Smith, Gordon Pincott and Dick Dodson.
6. McPheters, R. (1998) Researching print readers, *Admap*, September, pp 34–36.

Chapter 3

1. In the examples, a parabola or second degree curve is used, except for Christmas. A sine curve may be more appropriate, but is a bit more trouble to fit.

Chapter 4

1. Paul Dyson and Nigel Hollis have generously shared the data in these examples. Millward Brown modelling is not directly comparable with adstock modelling: see Brown, G. (1986) Modelling advertising awareness, *The Statistician*, **35**, pp 289–299. The decay normally used is 10 per cent per week.

    Note that this rate depends crucially on the actual question, 'Which of these brands of (product field) have you seen advertised on TV *recently*?' Decay is faster if they ask '...last night' or, '...in the last few days', and slower if the question is, '...ever seen?'

    This is a good example of the rule that the rate of decay depends on the prompt, i.e. *what* we measure. It may also depend here on the length of the prompt list and the amount of competitive pressure. Too often, non-researchers assume there is some tangible, constant entity to be measured. There is not – there are only different responses to different stimuli.

    The model additionally allows for diminishing returns. There is more in Chapter 12, and links between awareness and sales are described in Hollis, N. Television advertising: measuring short-term and long-term effects, in (1998) *How Advertising Works*, Ed. John Philip Jones, Sage Publications, Inc., pp 244–265.

2. A technical explanation is given on pp 153–166 of Broadbent, S. (1997) *Accountable Advertising*, Admap Publications. The parameter *d* used here is exactly the same as the 'fade parameter' *f* there.

3. See, among other papers, Deighton, J. *et al.* (1988) *Advertising Framing Effects in Field Data*, University of Chicago, Graduate School of Business, December, from which I take the following quotations. A more accessible reference is Deighton, J. and Schindler, R.M. (1988) Can advertising influence experience?, *Psychology and Marketing*, **5**, No 2, pp 103–115. 'Advertising ... causes the consumer to interpret the consumer's product experience as more rewarding than it would have been... Advertising might suggest to the consumer how to make sense of what he or she has just experienced, resolving ambiguities and influencing what is retained in memory.' The paper quotes a view on

shoppers' reactions: 'Advertising alone (is) untrustworthy; evidence alone (is) too difficult to interpret.'

4. McDonald, C. (1996) Advertising sales effects, *Admap*, April, pp 39– 43. In a comment on a draft of this book, McDonald wrote that he thinks we are really in agreement. 'I am thinking of response rather than sales effect. I can't believe that an ad which works, even in the long term, can do this without evoking some sort of response – even though it may not be possible for us to see it, it may not lead to any short-term action, the shopper may be quite unconscious of it. In this sense, I believe long and short term are the same, but the measurement of the sales results may well be very different. How the response affects sales may change over time, under the impact of competition, retail changes and most of all experience in using the brand.'

5. This is usually attributed to Hugh Zielske, but its first publication was by Pomerance, E. and Zielske, H. (1958) How frequently should you advertise?, *Media/Scope*, September. The usual source given is Zielske, H. (1959) The remembering and forgetting of advertising, *Journal of Marketing*, **23**, January, pp 239–243. The work was extended to a study of television and tracking scores, for six products or services from a total of 17 studies. Zielske, H. and Henry, W. (1980) Remembering and forgetting television ads, *Journal of Advertising Research*, **20**, No 2, April, pp 7–13. Similar conclusions were drawn.

6. Simon, J. (1979) What do Zielske's real data really show about pulsing?, *Journal of Marketing Research*, August, pp 415–420.

7. Simon quotes a dozen papers referring to the original, and there have been more since 1979. However, the work is probably as much remembered for the higher peak in awareness generated by the concentrated schedule and by the defence of the 'breakthrough' theory – the exact opposite of Simon's conclusion.

8. Broadbent, S. and Fry, T. (1995) Adstock modelling for the long term, *Journal of the Market Research Society*, **37**, pp 385–403.

9. Several analyses of this type have been published in various journals and other places, under the general heading *How TV Advertising Works*. The data selected for this description are from 'General truths? Nine key findings from IRI test data', Lodish, L.M. and Lubetkin, B. *Admap*, February 1992, pp 9–15. A fuller description was published later: Lodish, L.M. *et al.* (1995) A summary of fifty-five in-market experimental estimates of the long-term effect of TV advertising, *Marketing Science*, **14**, No. 3, pp G133–G140. This time 42 weight tests were analysed with results co-variantely adjusted for differences between advertised and non-advertised groups for price, display and promotion conditions. The percentage increases in sales volume over the

three years were essentially the same as in the text: 20.9, 14.3 and 8.0 per cent.

10. Hall, J. (1998) How advertising works 2, *European Advertising Effectiveness Symposium*, Advertising Seminars International.

11. Naik, P.A., Mantrala M., Sawyer A.G. (1998). Planning media schedules in the presence of dynamic advertising quality, *Marketing Science*, **17**, No 3, pp 214–235.

12. Fry, T., Broadbent, S. and Dixon, J. (1999) Estimating advertising half-life and the data interval bias, Department of Econometrics and Business Statistics Working Paper, June 1999, Monash University, Victoria, Australia. See also Leone, R. (1995) Generalising what is known about temporal aggregation and advertising carryover, *Marketing Science*, **14**, pp G141–G150.

Chapter 5

1. There used to be much debate about the shape. Most mentions of response functions describe the s-shape, and conclude that there might be a threshold below which advertising is uneconomic. This shape is certainly possible – for high values of the cover criterion (three or four, for example) the relation of cover to increasing GRPs has this shape. Erik Du Plessis has argued that not only products, but ads themselves start life with an s-shaped response to media weight. Hence, he says, if they are not husbanded through this period, and given sufficient weight or frequency, they will be ineffectual. There is also a tradition of introducing a new campaign with a burst heavier than normal, explained by this argument.

   There can be a threshold for GRPs themselves, in the sense that it is not worth making a film and going to the trouble of buying time if GRPs are too low.

   But a review over 30 years ago concluded that the convex shape was normal: Broadbent, S. and Segnit, S. (1967) Response functions in media planning. In *Ten Years of Advertising Media Research*, The Thomson Organisation (1972). So did one 20 years ago: Simon, J. and Arndt, J. (1980) The shape of the advertising response function, *Journal of Advertising Research*, **20**, No 4, August, pp 11–28. For an introduction and critical view, see McDonald, C. (1984) Whatever happened to response functions?, *Admap*, October, pp 460–465.

   Similar ideas have been applied in print. Repeated exposures had the following effects: significant changes at the first insertion, continued gain in later weeks, higher frequency produced greater gain, behaviour changed more than attitudes, low-awareness brands benefited more than high-awareness brands. *Time* Magazine and Seagrams (1982) *A Study of the Effectiveness of Advertising Frequency in Magazines.*

2. If the different conclusion from Zeno worries you, note that the times for the arrow get vanishingly small, whereas the OTS keep adding up indefinitely!

3. The equation for diminishing returns, at a rate of x OTS per week, or current adstock divided by 100, is y = (upper limit) times $1 - [1-F]x$ where F is the parameter explained in the text.

4. One output of a regression analysis is an estimate of how well determined are each of the coefficients which represent the sizes of the effects studied. This is given by a number called 't'. If this is large enough (roughly, over two) we know the size of the effect rather precisely.

    Another output is called 'R-squared', which tells us the proportion of the variation in the raw data 'explained' by the effects.

    When we try different fits (for example, varying the half-life for adstock), we see which is better by choosing the one with the largest t-value or giving the largest R-squared.

5. Broadbent, S. (1997) Single source – new analyses, *Journal of the Market Research Society*, **39**, April.

6. Zielske discarded a freak observation in week 5, so do I. The formula for diminishing returns is again: recall = maximum x $(1 - F)^{adstock/100}$, where I found that maximum = 95 and F = 0.8 gave a reasonable fit for both the concentrated and spread-out schedules.

7. This work was carried out for Starcom Media Services, Chicago, as part of a project called *113 Cases*.

Chapter 6

1. I quote Priemer several times, with admiration at his realism about the media process. The main reference is in Chapter 11.

2. See for a current view Spittler, J. (1998) TV optimisers: fad or trend?, *Admap*, September, pp 25–27, and for a view on reach as opposed to targeting, Ephron, E. (1998) The fog of battle, *Admap*, September, pp 28–30.

3. Broadbent, S. (1998) Effective frequency: there and back, *Admap*, May, pp 34–38.

4. See *Media Week*, September 13, 1996, pp 10–11.

5. This is not fanciful. Such a source can be constructed, though not with the official viewing panel as this cannot be tampered with. There is more in Chapters 9 and 11.

Chapter 7

1. This part of the solution was 'new' 20 years ago: Broadbent, S. (1981) A new approach to budget allocation over time, *Admap*, August, pp 382–392. The way of combining the budget, values, costs, previous GRPs, decay and diminishing returns into the 'effectiveness' of a schedule has not changed. What we thought then were typical half-lives – four to 16 weeks was quoted – are now much shorter. Some of the sales data then modelled were bi-monthly; weekly or daily data were very rare, and we did not know much about interval bias. Some of the fits might now be made with two half-lives – one short and one long.

   The main improvements in the current system are the ability to construct a schedule, and to allow when doing this for obligatory GRPs, which means we can write part of the schedule for one half-life, and allow for

   this when we use a different half-life. Another innovation is thinking about the cover criterion at the same time as scheduling. The ideas of minimum GRPs when on air, and of maximum GRPs follow naturally.
2. See McDonald, C. and King, S. (1996) *A Ballade of Multiple Regression in Sampling the Universe*, NTC Publications.

Chapter 8

1. Since this is a method I recommend, I describe the technique briefly. From the formula for response to changing ratings, we can derive the slope – how much response improves for a unit change in ratings. At the optimum allocation, these slopes must be the same in every region, or we could do better by taking from the flattest and giving to the steepest. So we have an equation for each region, setting the slope equal to some constant. For any constant, we know the slope, and therefore the spend in each region.

   There is a further condition, that total spend equals the budget. This is enough information for us to calculate the constant, and therefore the ratings in each region.
2. The example of Northland and Southshire is expanded here. The methods clearly generalise to any number of regions. The formulae are

derived, and examples given, in Broadbent, S. (1988) *The Advertiser's Handbook for Budget Determination*, Lexington Books.

First, the basic facts are repeated, and for this case I suppose we have sales data for the regions, otherwise 'value' would be calculated some other way:

	Population, homemakers, 000	Cost of 100 ratings	Category sales, 000	Brand sales, 000
Northland	1,500	10,674	1,400	400
Southshire	721	5,906	1,000	300
Total	2,221		2,400	700

From these we calculate some key numbers:

	Brand share	Brand Development Index (BDI)	Category Development Index (CDI)
Northland	28.6%	84.6	86.4
Southshire	30.0%	132.0	128.4

The indices show how well the brand, or the category, is doing in each region. This is worked out from sales per head, indexed on the national average. It now becomes clear that the category has much higher sales per head in Southshire, which may be a reason why it justifies higher cost per thousand impacts (you cannot see this from the cost per hundred ratings, since these also take the size of the region into account). The brand is also doing slightly better there.

From the table above, or from other sources, we now have to decide on the 'value' of a shopper in each region. This is a strategic decision, not a mechanical one. For example, if we expected category sales per head to increase in Northland for some reason, we would put up the value there. The numbers we settle on have no absolute meaning – they are used solely as indices. Suppose we decide on 90 and 130.

The Equal Impacts allocation does not need this decision. It is a particular case of ratings in proportion to values, which is worked out from the following table:

	Values	Costs for these ratings	Budget, £000
Northland	90	9,607	55,600
Southshire	130	7,678	44,400
Total		17,284	100,000

In the 'costs' column, I have worked out what it would cost to buy the entries in the 'values' column, if they were ratings. To satisfy the budget restriction, I then multiply the entries in the 'cost' column by 100,000 / 17,284.

If I do this sum with equal values for the two regions, the budget splits £64,400 and £35,600, giving 603 ratings in both regions.

Splitting the budget in proportion to population x values means that we first work out the product of populations and values, which is equivalent to the importance of the region, and then divide the budget in this proportion.

Introduction to Part 2

1. Feynam, R.P. (1988) *What do you Care what Other People Think?*, Unwin Hyman.

Chapter 9

1. Broadbent, S. and Segnit, S. (1967) *Response Functions in Media Planning*. Referred to in Chapter 5.
2. Broadbent, S. (1970) *Spending Advertising Money*, Business Books. In later editions, such as the fourth, in 1984, modelling was introduced to help the decision.
3. Anon (1993) *The First Sixty Years*. BMRB, London.
4. For example, Bird, M. and Ehrenberg, A.S.C. (1966) Intentions-to-buy and claimed brand usage, *Operations Research Quarterly*, **17**, pp 27–46 and **18**, pp 65–66, (1966) Non-awareness and non-usage, *Journal of Advertising Research*, **6**, pp 4–8.
5. Joyce, T. (1967) *Admap*, September.
6. McDonald, C. (1969) Relationships between advertising exposure and purchasing behaviour, *Market Research Society Conference*, pp 67–98.
7. Joyce, T. (1967) What do we know about how advertising works? ESOMAR. Reprinted in *Consumer Behaviour* (1971) Penguin, London, edited by Ehrenberg, A.S.C. and G. Pyatt.
8. For example, King, S. (1975) Practical progress from a theory of advertisements, *Admap*, October.
9. For example, an early paper is: Ehrenberg, A. (1974) Repetitive advertising and the consumer. *Journal of Advertising Research*, **14**, April, pp 26–34.

10. Bullmore, J. (1998) *Behind the Scenes in Advertising*, Second Edn, Admap Publications.
11. McDonald, C. (1970) What is the short term effect of advertising?, ESOMAR, reprinted in *Market Researchers Look at Advertising*, Ed. Broadbent, S. Sigmatext, pp 39–50.
12. Barnes, M. (1971) *The Relationships Between Purchasing Patterns and Advertising Exposure*, JWT, London.
13. Private communication from Colin McDonald.
14. Gullen, P. and Johnson, H. (1985) Effective frequency – how much is enough?, *Media World*, June, pp 26–29.
15. Colin McDonald (1999) Advertising response, effective frequency and single source data. In *Handbooks on Best Advertising Practice*, Vol. 4, edited by John Philip Jones, Sage Publications Inc. The project is described in Gullen, P. (1985) Planning media to create sales, *Admap*, October, pp 505–511.
16. Broadbent, S. (1986) Two OTS in a purchase interval – some questions, *Admap*, November, pp 12–15.
17. Moseley, S. and Parfitt, J. (1987) Measuring advertising effect from single source data: the first year of the AdLab panel, *Admap*, June, pp 26–32. Also, Moseley, S. (1997) Linking sales tracking data to television viewing, *Admap*, April, pp 62–65.

Chapter 10

1. Gus Priemer – I quote him several times, the main reference is in Chapter 11.
2. Many large companies used experiments – it was the accepted technique at the time and for years to come. See, for example, Eastlack, J.O. and Rao, A.G. (1989) Advertising experiments at the Campbell Soup Company, *Marketing Science*, **8**, 1. pp 57–77. A contemporary reference is Mayer, M. (1965) *The Intelligent Man's Guide to Sales Measures of Advertising*, Advertising Research Foundation, New York. This gives 32 references to papers reporting experiments, but also 45 where approved statistical analyses of various types were carried out. These are in addition to the 'disarmingly simple' studies where data as-they-fall show that people who buy more of the brand also have associations with its advertising.
3. Colley, R.H. (1961) *Defining Advertising Goals for Measured Advertising Results*, Association of National Advertisers Inc., New York.
4. Zealley, J. (1996) Admap Seminar, London.

5. Naples, M.J. (1973) Advertising '73: microscope or telescope?, ARF Annual Conference.

6. Naples, M.J. (1994) The effective frequency concept, ARF Effective Frequency Day.

7. Stewart, M.S. (1980) Measuring advertising effects by area tests, *Admap*, March. In the April issue he published results for 92 area tests: Was StatScan really an advance on AMTES?

8. Broadbent, S. (1970) *Spending Advertising Money*, Business Books, London.

9. Miller, H. (1978) Flighting – it's still the same old game, ANA Workshop, 2 March.

10. Naples, M.J. (1979) Effective frequency, Association of National Advertisers, New York.

11. Naples, M. (1997) Effective frequency: then and now, *Journal of Advertising Research*, July/August, pp 7–12.

12. Krugman, H. E. (1972) Why three exposures may be enough, *Journal of Advertising Research*, **12**, 6, December, pp 11–14.

13. Colin McDonald (1999) Advertising response, effective frequency and single source data. In *Handbooks on Best Advertising Practice*, **4**, edited by John Philip Jones, Sage Publications Inc.

14. Ramond, C. (1976) What we already know, *Journal of Advertising Research*, April, p 60.

15. Moran, W. (1976) Does flighting pay? ARF Annual meeting, New York, 19 October.

16. Moran, W. (1977) When to run, when to stop and flight, ANA Advertising Workshop, New York, 15 March.

17. Corkindale, D. and Newall, J. (1978) Advertising thresholds and wearout, *European Journal of Marketing*, **12**, 5, pp 327–378.

18. Rao, A.G. and Sablava D. J. (1986) Marketing Science Institute, Boston, pp. 86 – 105.

19 Leckenby, J.D. and Kim, H. (1994) How media directors view reach/frequency, *Journal of Advertising Research*, September/October.

20. Sissors, J. (1986) Advice to planners on how to use effective frequency. This was followed by ten papers by experts, all to a common list of questions. *Journal of Media Planning*, Fall, pp 3– 56.

21. The next four references are all from: *Advertising Research Foundation, Effective Frequency Day*. McDonald, C. (1994) Effective frequency, the relation between frequency and advertising effectiveness.

22. Achenbaum, A. (1994) Revising the original concept of effective frequency.

23. Bogart, L. (1994) Is there an optimum frequency in advertising?

24. Evanson, D. (1994) Media plans ineffectively use effective frequency.

25. Kaplan, R. (1989) How many times should you run your ad?, *Inside Print*, March, pp 25–29.

26. McDonald, C. (1995) *Advertising Reach and Frequency: Maximising Advertising Results Through Effective Frequency*, NTC Business Books with the Association of National Advertisers, New York.

27. Jones, J.P. (1995) *When Ads Work*, Lexington Books, New York.

Chapter 11

1. Weinblatt & Douglas (1992). Their proposal to replace the push-button personal TV meter was for a watch worn by the viewer which stores the programme codes transmitted with TV.

2. Shababb, G. (1992) True winners – using single source to allocate TV time, *Admap*, February, pp 26–30.

3. Jones, J.P. (1995) *When Ads Work*, Lexington Books. Unspecified references below are all to this book.

4. See p 9.

5. Jones, J.P. (1995) Yes, we have a breakthrough, *Admap*, June, pp 33–35, in response to a review I wrote in the same issue.

6. See pp xv, 44 and 46.

7. This ought to be the definition of STAS, which averages 124 above, but the book is clear, on p 44, that 114 is meant.

8. Jones, J.P. (1997) What does effective frequency mean in 1997?, *Journal of Advertising Research*, July/August, pp 14–20.

9. McDonald, C. (1997) Short term advertising effects: how confident can we be?, *Admap*, June, pp 36–39. This paper also points out that STAS can be broken down into two statistics which he had previously defined, called Change and Repeat, depending on the brand bought in the previous purchase.

10. An early reference is Anderson, T. and Zelditch, M. (1958) *A Basic Course in Statistics*, Holt, Rinehart and Winston.

11. This is for the UK in 1998: (1998) *Redefining Media Evaluation*, TSMS and Taylor Nelson Sofres.

12. The 1998 MRI Doublebase data was used.

13. See also McDonald, C. (1997) From 'frequency' to 'continuity' – is it a new dawn?, *Journal of Advertising Research*, July/August. pp 21–25. This reports the Adlab analysis in yet another way, with the conclusion that 'STAS cannot simply be taken at face value'. It is also a concise review of his own work on the 1996 data and on his rewrite of Mike Naples' book.

14. One factor in the UK which leads to advertised brands having a higher share among heavy viewers is the preference light viewers show for buying stores' Own Label products, even across social grades.
15. Buck, S. (1994) Pressures on premium brands: the role of TV advertising, ITV, London. 'Any OTS' is the heading Jones used, though it has incorrectly appeared as the expected '2 + OTS', as in Jones, J.P. (1995) Advertising exposures under the microscope, *Admap*, February, pp 28–31.
16. The one summarised here is titled *So wirkt Werbung in Deutschland*, by John Philip Jones, Burckhard Brandes, who was running Nielsen in Germany, and Peter Haller who was running GWA. The other two are titled *Wie man den Erfolg der Werbung mißt* and *Media werbung contra Verkaufsförderung* and do not concern us here, as they mainly repeat the US book with German comment.
17. See p 202.
18. See p 60.
19. See p 28.
20. The entry 25 is from 19 on p 101 and 6 on p 116; 31 is from 26 on p 85 and 5 on p 116; 10 is from 3 on p 116 and 7 on p 129. The remainder of the entries follow from these.
21. I am grateful to Alan Smith for pointing out a review and update of this work: Napior, D. and Bailey, J. (1998) NetAPPs: Daniel Starch's method for measuring Net Ad Produced Purchases, ARF Workshop, New York, October. Starch was well aware of doubts about the validity of such measures. He used a variety of them, and wrote extensively on the subject: Starch, D. (1996) *Measuring Advertising Readership and Results*, McGraw Hill. More in the notes on Chapter 12.
22. Leslie Wood reported on an early version of the AdImpact measure in October 1989, at a TV Audience Symposium. Work with Nielsen data started in March 1991. The two analysts met Jones in March 1992. See also Papazian, E. (1992) New scanner-based analysis system tracks sales results for TV ad campaigns, *Marketsense*, May.
23. This is the normal statistical procedure – see the work by Roberts in Chapter 12.
24. Reichel, W. (1994) Beyond 'effective frequency': how to maximise marketplace impact using new data-based approaches to media scheduling, *Effective Frequency Day*, ARF.
25. Reichel, W. and Wood, L. (1997) Recency in media planning – redefined, *Journal of Advertising Research*, July/August, pp 66–74: this has been amplified in a personal communication.
26. In this case, for up to two days before, the sales effect at 2+ was 11, hardly between 27 and 17.

27. Priemer, A.B. (1989) *Effective Media Planning*, Lexington Books. This remarkable book is not recommended for those of a nervous disposition. His views of the 'conventional media ritual', as he calls it, are unfavourable and unrestrained. It is not surprising that he was such an influence for good on Ephron and doubtless on many others who shared his passion for common sense and ruthless logic.

28. Ephron, E. (1992) The rule of three?, *Inside Media*, 8 January.

29. Ephron, E (1995) More weeks, less weight: the shelf-space model of advertising. *Journal of Advertising Research*, May–June, pp 18–23.

30. Bogart, L., Tolley, B.S. and Orenstein, F. (1970) What one little ad can do, *Journal of Advertising Research*, **10**, 4, pp 3–13.

31. Gibson, L. (1996) What can one TV exposure do?, *Journal of Advertising Research*, March/April, pp 9–18.

32. *The Myers Report*, on 16 December, 1996, commented on the 'Ephron Factor'. Research established that the majority of major national advertisers and agency media professionals are not only aware of recency planning but are strongly inclined to adopt it. A study of the schedules of some major advertisers confirms that in 1997 they indeed advertised in more weeks. See Ephron, E. (1998) The new 'recency' planning, *Media Week*, 16 March, p 14; also Ephron. E. (1997) Recency planning, *Journal of Advertising Research*, July–August, pp 61–64, as well as many conference papers.

33. Ephron, E. (1996) The Bible, lately revised, *Inside Media*, January 10. p 22.

34. Broadbent, S. and Ephron, E. (1999) Two views of scheduling – how far apart?, *Admap*, January, pp 22–25. Also at the Americas Conference, ARF, May 1999.

35. Ephron, E. (1998) Bringing recency planning to magazines, ARF Workshop, October.

Chapter 12

1. An early example was Broadbent, S. (1995) Single source – the breakthrough?, *Admap*, June, pp 29–33, to which Jones responded in the same issue.

2. Livanas, R. (1996) Is once really enough for an effective ad?, *Research*, Sydney, Australia, May.

3. Tenbusch, A. (1998) What are we learning of the relationship between advertising and promotions?, *European Advertising Effectiveness Symposium*, Advertising Seminars International.

4. Schroeder, G., Richardson, B. and Sankaralingham, A. (1996) Investigating the validity of the short term advertising strength (STAS) concept using BehaviorScan, ARF Electronic Marketing Research Technology Workshop, May, New York. See also, by the same authors, (1997) Validating STAS using BehaviorScan, *Journal of Advertising Research*, New York, July/August.

5. Kindelman, K. and Wildner, R. (1997) What a revised STAS can tell us about advertising's short term effects, *The European Advertising Effectiveness Symposium*, Advertising Seminars International.

6. Jones, J.P. and Blair, M.H. (1996) Examining conventional wisdom about advertising effects with evidence from independent sources, *Journal of Advertising Research*, **36**, 6, pp 37–59.

7. Lodish, L.M. (1997) J.P. Jones and M.H. Blair on measuring advertising effects – another point of view, *Journal of Advertising Research*, September/October, pp 75–79.

8. Jones, J.P. (1998) STAS and BehaviorScan – yet another view, and Lodish, L.M. (1998) STAS and BehaviorScan – it's just not that simple, *Journal of Advertising Research*, March/April, pp 51–53 and 54–56.

9. Battais, L. and Spitzer, L. (1996) The French single source experience, ESOMAR Seminar, Rome, November, pp 209–218.

10. For example, in the *Journal of Advertising Research*, special issue in July/August 1997, see the papers by Longman and by Gonten and Donius. Also, Franz, G. (1998) Making marketing communication accountable by market modelling, *The 1998 European Advertising Effectiveness Symposium*, Hamburg, Advertising Seminars International.

11. Canter, N. (1998) Pragmatic approaches from the USA, *Modeller's Workshop*, TN-Sofres, London, May. I am also grateful to Bob Wyman for permission to quote from a description of the process.

12. See *Admap* between 1976 and 1987, where there are 19 papers by O'Herlihy. Scheduling over time is a major part of this work and more continuity is often argued for.

13. See, for example, Dyson, P. (1996) Media planning case history – using modelling to improve media laydown, *Admap*, December, and Dyson, P. (1998) Justifying the advertising budget, *Admap* and Advertising Association Conference, January.

14. Paul Dyson, personal communication.

15. Because, when the base is zero, the non-aware fraction, (1–F)/100, is here 0.8. Squaring this gives 0.64 so the new awareness is 100(1–0.64) or 36 per cent. The third OTS means the non-awareness proportion is 0.83, so awareness is 48.8 per cent, and so on, geometrically.

16. Broadbent, S. (1997) Single source – new analyses, *Journal of the Market Research Society*, **39**, 2, pp 363–379. For the scheduling implications, see Broadbent, S., Spittler, J. and Lynch, K. (1997) Building better TV schedules: new light from the single source, *Journal of Advertising Research*, July–August, pp 27–31.

17. Tellis, G.T. (1997) Effective frequency: one exposure or three factors?, *Journal of Advertising Research*, July–August, pp 75–80.

18. This is the 'Penrith Project', by Carat Research, summarised, for example, in Hone, L. (1995) Three strikes is out, *Media Week*, 16 June, p 12.

19. Isaac, T.G. and Milnes, B. (1996) The Holy Grail at a bargain basement price?, *ESOMAR Seminar, Managing Media Data for Market Profit*, Rome, pp 227–239.

20. The reader may be surprised by the number of different indices which may be used to measure association in a simple 2x2 table – I know of a dozen. We here have Roberts' as well as Reichel's and Jones'. The Starch numbers mentioned in Chapter 11 provide others. One of Starch's has been applied by Jones under the heading 'Single Issue Readership Method' and unfortunately the phrase 'STAS Differential Index' is used, though this is not STAS. See Jones, J.P. (1998) Does STAS only work with television advertising?, *Telmar Awards Paper*, New York, April. All the indices are different ways of describing how many more occasions or informants there are, both exposed to advertising and choosing the brand, than expected if these two were independent. They are also all related to each other. More in Broadbent, S. and Smith, A. (1999) Use of the 2-by-2 table in advertising effectiveness research, *Marketing and Research Today*, May, pp 45–51.

21. Roberts, A. (1997) Optimising advertising and promotions, *The 1997 European Advertising Effectiveness Symposium*, Paris, Advertising Seminars International.

22. Roberts, A. (1998) TVSpan, recency, frequency and the duration of the sales effects of TV advertising, Taylor Nelson Sofres, November, or more accessibly (1999) Recency, frequency and the sales effects of advertising, *Admap*, February, pp 40–44.

23. Popper, K. (1988) *Postscript to the Logic of Scientific Discovery*, **2**, Open University, Routledge.

24. Private communication. For an earlier comment, see Roberts, A. (1996) What do we know about advertising's short term effects?, *Admap*, February. Note that these are overall summaries, but Roberts prefers to look within weights of viewing, where linearity is more likely, as shown earlier.

Index